William Henry Platt

After Death

Hell and Salvation Considered in the Light of Science and Philosophy. Second

Edition

William Henry Platt

After Death

Hell and Salvation Considered in the Light of Science and Philosophy. Second Edition

ISBN/EAN: 9783337253165

Printed in Europe, USA, Canada, Australia, Japan

Cover: Foto ©Lupo / pixelio.de

More available books at **www.hansebooks.com**

AFTER DEATH–WHAT?

OR

Hell and Salvation

Considered in the Light of Science and Philosophy.

BY

REV. W. H. PLATT,

Rector of Grace Church, San Francisco.

Second Edition—Revised and Enlarged.

From three Lectures delivered in Grace Church, San Francisco, January 13th, 20th, 27th, 1878.

SAN FRANCISCO:
A. ROMAN & CO., PUBLISHERS.
1878.

BACON & COMPANY, PRINTERS,
Excelsior Office, Corner Clay and Sansome Streets,
San Francisco.

ERRATA.

Page vii, sixth line, for *true* read *brute*.

Page 3, twelfth line, for *matter* read *Being*.

Page 15, seventh line, for *religion* read *science*.

Page 83. The fifth paragraph on this page should read: "I suppose," remarked the preacher, "as Büchner says that, I ought to understand what it means," etc.

TO THE

Congregation of Grace Church,

SAN FRANCISCO,

This Volume

Is Affectionately Dedicated by

THEIR PASTOR.

CONTENTS.

I.—PAIN (*Punishment*) AS AN EFFECT OF VIOLATED LAW.
1. Is the human soul immortal?
    (*a.*) Immortality through *the persistence of type.*
    The human type.
    The true type.
    (*b.*) Immortality through *the persistence of consciousness.*
    Consciousness essentially not matter.
    Consciousness survives as the fittest.
    (*c.*) Immortality through *the persistence of force.*
    The human mind as force.
    The brute mind as force.
    Brutes individuals, not persons.
2. The Law of Affinity proves a Hell.
3. The Law of Association proves it.
4. The Law of Growth proves it.
5. The Law of Propagation proves it.
6. The Law of Involution proves it.
7. The Law of Evolution proves it.

II.—PAIN (*Punishment*) USED AS A PRESENT MEANS BY GOD THE FATHER.
1. False Ideas of the Fatherhood of God.
2. True Ideas of the Fatherhood of God.
    (*a.*) God uses Pain as a Present Teacher.
    (*b.*) God uses Pain as a Present Corrective.
    (*c.*) God uses Pain as a Present Restraint.

III.—PAIN (*Punishment*) ENDLESS AS A RESULT OF CHARACTER—MAN'S OWN ACT.

IV.—SALVATION, GOD'S ACT IN ONE OF THREE WAYS.
   1. As a Destiny.
      (*a.*) Universal at Death.
      (*b.*) Universal by Final Restoration.
   2. As an Achievement of Man.
   3. As a Gift from Christ.
V.—THE SKEPTIC AS A MOURNER.

After Death—What?

I.

Pain (*Punishment*) Considered as an Evolved Effect of Impersonal Law.

Let me give an outline of a symposium or conversation that is not altogether imaginary, between a christian preacher and a skeptical scientist. Instead of skepticism being diffident of its doubts, it is now confident and obtrusive. The scientist boldly asks the preacher why he continues to preach the old fashioned hell. " Do you not know," he says, "that intelligent people now laugh at your lake of fire and brimstone, your devil with horns and dragon tail, and all that sort of stuff?"

"The Bible," says the preacher, "proves ____."

"Nothing to me," interrupted the skeptic; "the science of nature is the only revelation that we can trust. The critical study of the Bible has revealed its many glaring inconsistencies."

" Only to those," replied the preacher, "who wish and are resolved to find or make them. Hitherto, until the revival of bald materialism, those who have known the most about nature, such as Copernicus, Newton and Agassiz, have believed the most about the Bible and God. Even now, in England, ' out of every ten scientific men, seven call themselves members of the established churches of England, Scotland, or of the now disestablished church of Ireland; and two belong to the sects. Only one belongs to no church.' [1]

" Religion is not alarmed because science can explain so much, but because, with its thousand and one theories, it can explain so little. The more true knowledge, the more enlightened belief. And what can we trust in the con-

[1] "Men of Science," by Galton, p. 95.

clusions of material science, as to questions above matter, more than in statements of revelation ? How inconsistent are your theories of nature ! No two physicians agree as to the cause, phase, or treatment of disease ; no two scientists—— "

" And no two theologians," sarcastically interposed the skeptic, " agree about dogmas."

" If you scientists differ about finite matter, which you can see," replied the preacher, " is it remarkable that we theologians should differ about infinite mattter, which we cannot see ? Materialism neither explains matter, proposes a morality, or admits an accountability for conduct. Christian theologies may differ, but their moral aim is one. If both theology and materialism are uncertain, let us choose that which leads to the best life. The blindnes of us theologians does not make you scientists see. If science is required for the practical arts, so is Bible wisdom necessary to form moral character and social relations. Neither chemistry nor a knowledge of the multiplication table can make men morally better. ' The intellect has no morality.' You explore matter by the crucible, the scales, and the scalpel. We prove the principles of religion and the claim of revelation by the purity of the domestic relations which they appoint, the elevation of personal character which they effect, and the best moral movements of the world, which they inspire. If God can write chronologies of physical changes on the rocks, why can he not write rules of conduct elsewhere and in human language? But, as you object to the authority of revelation, I propose to prove by your own admitted principle of science, that there is a local hell."

"You certainly cannot look me in the face," replied the skeptic, "and say that you can prove, by any evidence respected by science, that there is, hereafter, a local hell? If there be such a place, where is it?"

"It is where the incorrigible sinner is, anywhere and everywhere, out of heaven. Surely that is place enough. But the reality is more important than the place. Locality is not essential to suffering," replied the preacher; "but not to evade the question, I undertake to prove, by principles of science admitted by you, that there is a local hell."

"And you agree to put in the brimstone, too?" ejaculated the skeptic.

"If not that, something worse," replied the preacher. "When you have heard me through, you will yourself prefer the brimstone."

"You are jesting, surely. Anyhow, the brimstone is only figurative fuel."

"The figure never equals the fact. Figures of speech are only used when plain language would fail to convey a full impression of the truth. The conclusions of science establish a hell in fact to which the figurative one of lake and brimstone is a cool luxury."

"Are you in earnest?" inquired the skeptic, "or is this jesting?"

"There is no jest in the subject," answered the preacher; "and suffering in mind or body is no jest; nor is a mistake in this matter a jest. It is a question upon which neither nature, in her inexorable arrangement of things, nor humanity in its wailing *miserere*, can afford to jest."

"All that is very pretty preaching," remarked the skeptic; "but let us come to business."

"Agreed."

"How can you prove the hell of which you so confidently speak?"

"First," said the preacher, "let me ask, even at the risk of being diverted for the time into several side questions, if you, a Pyrrhonist, denying everying and affirming nothing, acknowledge any authority in religion or science?"

"I believe in the authority of science, and care not a fig about religion."

"What do you understand by science?" asked the preacher.

"Science," answered the skeptic, "is simply knowledge classified, systematized, made orderly, impersonal, and exact, instead of being left unclassified, fragmentary, personal, and inexact. Comte calls it common sense methodized and extended.[1] It is, first, a logic of search applicable to all departments of knowledge; and, secondly, a doctrine or body of

---

[1] Lewes, August No. Popular Science Monthly, 1878, p. 413.

truths and hypotheses, embracing the results of search."[1]

"Then," said the preacher, "we ask you to study the science of religion."

"But," said the skeptic, "religion is not a science, because its test is faith, and not reason."

"The test of this as of all other science," replied the preacher, "is both faith and reason."

"But the faith of theology and the faith of science are very different in their *credentials*," answered the skeptic.[2]

"Wherein do they differ?" asked the preacher.

"The former is a reliance on the truth of principles handed down by tradition, of which no verification is possible, no examination permissible," was the reply.

"Exactly the reverse is true," interposed the preacher. "By their fruits shall ye know them. Religion is not a theory, but is above

[1] Lewes, August No. Popular Science Monthly, 1878, p. 413.
[2] Ibid.

all else a practice and a life. Each one must make the experimental test in and for himself, and only for himself. A friend may possibly be found to atone for man's unholiness, but every man must seek to be holy in himself. Unlike material science, where the tests can be made only by those of special skill, the tests of religion can and must be made by the most uneducated, each one for himself. Every principle of religion is verifiable in the individual experience of man and the history of civilization; and each man has the credential in himself.[1]

"It is you scientists who are credulous. There are no superstitions that are so superstitious as the superstitions of scientific men.[2] Science has its faith, impossible of verification, no less than religion. At most, only the facts of science can be verified, not scientific opinion. How often do scientists hold quite different opinions on the same fact of nature."

[1] 'O, make but trial of His love,
Experience will decide
How blest are they, and only they,
Who in His truth confide.'

[2] Beard, Pop. Sci. Monthly, July, 1878, p. 338.

"It is true," admitted the skeptic, "we believe in the law of gravitation, though we individually have never opened the 'Principia,' and could not understand it if we did; but we rely upon those who can understand it, and who have found its teachings in harmony with fact. We believe in the measurement of the velocity of light, though ignorant of the methods by which the velocity is measured. We trust those who have sought and found. If we distrust them, the search is open to us as to them. The mariner trusts to the indications of the compass, without pretending to know how these indications were discovered, but assured by constant experience that they guide the ship safely. Its credentials are conformity with experience."[1]

"The same are the credentials of religion," replied the preacher. "By their fruits shall ye know them." "Whoso doeth my will shall know of the doctrine. Faith is shown by works."

[1] George Henry Lewes, in August No. Popular Science Monthly, p. 416.

"The credentials of religious truth are the same and as certain as those of scientific truth. Again, I ask, wherein do they differ? Both are established by the law of sufficient reason. Reasoning inductively, you prove by combustion the existence of an invisible element you call oxygen. Reasoning inductively, we prove by the phenomena before our eyes the existence of an invisible Creator, we call God. What do you know of your so-called evolutionary power, that we do not know of our creating God? We both reason *a posteriori*, from effects back to cause. The logic and the credentials are the same."

"What," asked the skeptic, "are your credentials of the so-called miracles?"

"What are the credentials of any past scientific experiment and discovery?" answered the preacher. "We accept the *statement* of past events or acts of individuals in the history of religion, as you do similar statements in the history of science, upon credible testimony. They admit of no other verification in either case. The testimony of the witnesses to the miracles is sustained by the strongest possible corroboration. I know of no valid answer to Paley's proposition, 'that there is satisfactory evidence that many, pretending to be original witnesses of the Christian miracles, passed their lives in labors, dangers, and sufferings, voluntarily undertaken and undergone in attestation of the accounts which they delivered, and solely in consequence of their belief of the truth of those accounts, and that they submitted, from the same motive, to new rules of conduct.' No other proof is possible, or necessary. If it is not believed, no proof would be, though the witness rose from the dead to offer it. The denial of its sufficiency indicates a mind not open to conviction; and all I can say is, that the responsibility of rejecting it is yours, not mine. We test eternal *principles* in religion as you do fundamental principles in nature, by experience and observation, but with this difference: you necessarily must take many principles upon the authority of others, whereas each man can and must test the whole of religious truth in and for himself. Those who have made experimental tests in both religion and physical science, and have died, cannot be brought to the stand as living witnesses; but they have, in both cases alike, left directions to the world how to verify, each for himself, whether the statement of principles they make be true or not. The teachings of the Bible imploringly urge mankind to prove them by experimental tests. The tests of science involve no change of moral conduct, but those of religion do, and there is the rub. For this reason, they will neither make experiments in religious science, nor credit the testimony of those who do. History, both biographical and political, records the tests, but you refuse to verify them. With verification unattempted, why should you reject the doctrines of Paul in religion, and accept, without verification, those of Newton in science?"

"But the teachings of Newton have been verified, and can be by any one."

"And the doctrines of Paul have been verified, and can be by any one. No, no! the secret is, that the verification of religious principles is for the heart and conscience, and affects conduct; while that of the principles of science is for the intellect, and requires no moral self-discipline."

"Do you think," asked the skeptic," that history," especially mediæval, will verify your claim for religion? You had the world all to yourself, and why did you not do more for civilization?"

"Religion will accept the moral balance sheet of civilization. Give it its credits, and it will stand by its debits. If you plank over a field of sprouting wheat, you can expect no harvest. Give religion as favorable conditions as you demand for science, and it will produce corresponding fruits. Environment is for religion as much as for science. At all times, the best influence as to conduct was and is religion. Science claims no influence whatever over conduct or the organization of society. It is at most, knowledge, not authority. If, in the middle ages, religion did not advance society as much as you think it ought to have done, you must show what could have advanced it more."

"Science would have done better, if you would have let it," replied the skeptic.

"Please specify a little," remarked the preacher.

"Did you not crush out philosophy?" asked the skeptic.

"Draper says it died a natural death," replied the preacher.

"Certainly he does not say so in his 'Conflict between Religion and Science,'" said the skeptic.

"That book of Draper's," replied the preacher, "is most discreditable to his literary honesty. There is hardly a speaking acquaintance between the title and the text. The title is 'Conflict between Religion and Science.' In the preface, he says: 'I have had little to say respecting the two great Christian confessions, the Protestant and Greek churches. As to the latter, it has never, since the restoration of science, arrayed itself in opposition to the advancement of knowledge. On the contrary, it has always met it with welcome. * * * In speaking of Christianity, reference is generally made to the Roman Church. None of the Protestant churches has ever occupied a position so imperious, none has ever had such widespread political influence. For the most part, they have been averse to constraint.' He should then have called his book a conflict between religion and the Roman Church. But that is a worn-out discussion, and such a title would not sell the book so well. In his ' Intellectual Development of Europe,' he opens his sixth chapter, by saying : ' It is a melancholy picture I have to present—the *old age* and death of Greek philosophy. The strong man of Aristotelianism and Stoicism is sinking into the supernatural dotard. * * * In this closing scene, no more do we find the vivid faith of Plato, the mature intellect of Aristotle, the manly self-control of Zeno. Greek philosophy is ending in garrulity and mysticism. It is leaning for help on the conjurer, juggler and high priest of nature. * * * The Roman soldier is about to take the place of the thinker. * * * Under the shadow of the Pyramids, Greek philosophy was born. After many wanderings, for a thousand years, round the shores of the Mediterranean, it came back to its native place, and under the shadow of the Pyramids, it died.' Remember, Draper admits that philosophy, which then was synonymous with science and all learning, died of old age. It did not die in any conflict with religion. Religion had nothing to do with its death, though much to do in supplying its place."

"Any way," said the skeptic, "the old creed and religion must give way. There is just as certainly a change in the whole religious thought of the race, as the sun shines. Doctrines taught fifty years ago are neither taught now as they then were, nor believed as they then were believed."[1]

"Which doctrine is to be changed?" asked the preacher. "Will you change the preceptive, historical, esthetical, or social element? Are not the Ten Commandments all right? What will you change in the Lord's Prayer? In the Sermon on the Mount? In the Promises? What will you change in this sentence: 'God,

[1] Beecher's Lecture, S. F., Aug. 24, 1878.

who is rich in mercy?' What will you change in this sentence: 'God so loved the world that He gave His only begotten Son to die, that whoso believeth in Him should not perish, but have everlasting life?' In what theological seminary, in what system of divinity, in what Articles of Faith, are they taught differently now from what they were fifty years ago, whether in America or England? The change is in your own mind only. Theological teaching is unchanged by those who teach theology at all. To deny is not to modify. Truth is denied now, as it ever has been, and ever will be."

"When science," says the skeptic, "has fairly mastered the principles of moral relations, as it has mastered the principles of physical relations, all knowledge will be incorporated in an homogeneous doctrine, rivaling that of the old theologies in its comprehensiveness, and surpassing it in the authority of its credentials. Christian ethics will then no longer mean ethics founded on the principles of christian theology, but on the principles expressing the social relations and duties of men in christianized society. Then, and not till then, will the conflict between theology and science finally cease." [1]

"Christianized society," said the preacher, "is formed by social relations and duties, originated in and animated by Christian theology. All theology is only a system of truth, announced in part by revelation, and accepted and certified by reason and experience. You set up the name—theology—only to quarrel with it. Theology is simply knowledge about the cause of things, systematized and classified, whether you derive that knowledge from nature or revelation. You evolutionary scientists have a theology so far as you admit a Power, personal or impersonal; and your impersonal-power-science is no more verifiable than the theology based upon a personal Being. In brief, religion knows as much of its God as science knows of its Cause. There is a point, almost anywhere towards the beginning of things, where science confesses it knows nothing, and can verify nothing: such as what is

[1] Lewes, Popular Science Monthly, August, 1878, p. 420.

matter, what is mind, what is the connection between the two, what is light, what is gravitation? The conjectures of science are as numerous as the phases of religious faith. One great difference is, that the faith of religion leads to good conduct, while the conjectures of science leave us in spiritual despair. The knowledge of religion is as classified, exact, and verifiable as that of science."

"As Darwin says,[1] 'so profound is our ignorance, and so high our presumption,' that I ask, what can we trust in the assumption of material science as to the origin and destiny of things, more than to the statements of the Bible, which we accept as revelations? Your theories of nature change with every teacher, and the last is presented as true by showing that those before it were false. How long has it been since Newton's emission theory of light, now discarded, was accepted as scientific certainty? Winchell says that 'progressive knowledge implies much unlearning.' When will scientific opinion be so complete and

[1] Origin of Species, Chap. III.

verified, and with credentials so certain, that the progress and happiness of the world will need no religious faith?"

"Science claims to be verifiable knowledge, and we all wish it could verify itself more than it does; but how limited is the range of what we really do know, and how unlimited the boundaries of what we do not know! Religion, more than science, mourns over the insignificance of human knowledge; but while science stops in despair at the operation of natural laws in this world, religion, accepting the doctrine of the eternal continuity of law, follows them on, in hope, into the next. The more light in science, more will be the light in religion. Let us have light around us, above us, and within us. Darkness is perilous. Science builds bridges, but they fall, killing thousands. It sends out fleets upon the ocean, but they sink. Pestilences come, and medicine fails. Ignorance leaves all men to die. Nature is as inscrutable now, as in the ages past. Then, as we have no science that can avert death here, let us not reject a religion that reveals to us a rescue from it hereafter. Science now claims that it has divorced superstition from religion. Let us hope that it is so. But, rejecting moral responsibility, the mystery of nature and blind law is put by the materialist for the mystery of a God and His providence. For the hope of faith, we have the despair of skepticism. Is the eternity of matter less a mystery than the eternity of God? And is not what we call science as ignorant of one as the other? Science is as blind to that which is behind us, as it is to that which is before us. 'It is incumbent upon us evolutionists,' says one,[1] 'to prove our opinion; yet, it must be admitted that, at present, we are far from having established a connected chain of evidence in support of it.' Instead of future immortality to be hoped for, we are offered, as the conclusion of science, a future of annihilations which cannot be proved. Science becomes unscientific in speaking confidently where it must be ignorant, and should be silent. With a wise

[1] Dr. Montgomery's Art. Monera, Pop. Sci. Monthly, Aug., 1878.

and more modest spirit, Virchow, speaking recently to a most learned assembly in Munich, said of the theory of spontaneous generation and the descent of man : 'We ought to say: Do not take this for established truth. Be prepared to find it otherwise. Only for the moment we are of opinion that it *may* be true.' We know the universe but in part ; and in the uncertain, limited, inexact, and variable results of all investigations, there is no such thing as science. Theory is not knowledge. Assumption is not proof. Words are not facts. Speculations are not laws."

"Is it not a law that heat expands all bodies and cold contracts them ?" asked the skeptic.

"No," replied the preacher ; " India-rubber contracts under heat, and water, below thirty-nine and one-half degrees, instead of contracting actually expands, as we all know from our broken pitchers on a very cold morning. Jevons[1] declares that it would be easy to point out an almost *infinite* number of other unexplained anomalies."

[1] Principles of Science, Vol. II, p. 341.

"You venture upon a very bold position, to say that there is no science," remarked the skeptic.

"Let us see," said the preacher. "What do you mean by science?"

"A provable knowledge of nature and of man," answered the skeptic.

"That I supposed would be your answer. But your mistake is in speaking of science as knowledge; whereas it is only a method to acquire knowledge," remarked the preacher. "You scientists agree upon nothing. In whatever direction you look, there is speculation, disagreement, and confusion. As to social institutions, Daniel Webster said :[1] 'For my part, though I like investigations of political questions, I give up what is called the science of political economy. There is no such science. There are no rules so fixed and invariable as that their aggregate constitutes a science. I believe that I have recently run over twenty volumes; and from the whole, if I should pick out with one hand all the mere truisms, and

[1] Bixby on Physical and Religious Knowledge, p. 170.

with the other all the doubtful propositions, little would be left.' In chemistry there is great disagreement. There is now a controversy going on in the papers, between the city engineers and the boards of health, as to the gravity of sewer gases. One opinion is that they are light, and rise up into houses in spite of traps and other plumbing devices. Others, among whom is the chief engineer of New York, as reported by the papers, contend that unhealthy gases are the heaviest and sink to the lowest points, as shown by disease in the lower localities of cities.[1] As to metrical systems of all kinds, it is only the simpler things that are open to even approximate measurement.[2] In the simplest natural phenomena, therefore, there will always be numberless factors whose exact influence can never be ascertained. Until we know thoroughly the nature

---

[1] The Pacific Medical and Surgical Journal for September, 1878, contains an article attacking the theory commonly received among physicians of the vegetable origin of malarious diseases, and arguing that the cause is to be found in the exposure of the body at night to cold, without proper covering and preparation, thus causing a chill and a suppression of the cutaneous secretions.

[2] Bixby, 174.

of matter, and the forces which produce its motions, says Thomson and Tait, it will be utterly impossible to submit to mathematical reasoning the exact conditions of any physical question.[1] Even physical astronomy, where the nearest approximation to actual conditions is found, is full of assumptions and neglect of numberless discrepancies. It is assumed in it, that the other millions of existing systems exert no perturbing influence on our system; that the planets are perfect ellipsoids, with absolutely smooth surfaces and homogenous interiors: assumptions, part of them, certainly untrue, as every hill and mountain show, and the rest very doubtful. In regard to other branches of science, the same thing is true. Scientific investigators speak and calculate about homogeneous substances, perfect fluids and gases, inflexible bars, etc., etc., but in reality there are no such things in nature.[2] We cannot, as Dr. W. O. Johnson recently warned his medical brethren, describe the commonest chemical change going on in the body; we cannot define

[1] Bixby, 174.   [2] Ibid.

the simplest of the vital processes. In the words of the chemist Berthollet, 'we know nothing of them thoroughly, since a perfect knowledge of any one of them involves a perfect knowledge of all the laws and forces which combine to produce it.'[1] Where is there an absolute standard measure of either direction, time, weight, or extension? What thorough knowledge or science is there of language, its origin, unity, structure, and elements? What two lexicographers pronounce alike? How differently words are spelled! Gould Brown, in his 'Grammar of Grammars,' tears all other grammarians utterly to pieces. No two physicians agree. 'The glorious uncertainty of the law' is proverbial. It is scarcely possible to find unanimity upon any legal proposition."

"Are the standards of religion less variable?" inquired the skeptic.

"That is not the question," replied the preacher. Those who live in glass houses should not throw stones. You claim to know when you do not. You allege the uncertainties

[1] Bixby, 175.

UNCERTAINTIES OF SCIENCE. 27

of religion, while your own uncertainties are greater. You would tear down the altars of religious faith, when you worship at darker ones of your own. You would close the doors of the churches, but how much do you open the doors of nature? You give the world a few variable, uncertain, and inexact rules of the practical arts, while you seek to persuade it that religion offers none for moral conduct. While the only certain truths are mental intuitions, such as those of mathematics, you teach the world that matter is the preëminent object of study. You pretend to prepare man for life only, whereas he needs to be first prepared for death; but you fail, in fact, to provide for either. But as you believe only in science, to science we will go."

"And not use your Bible?"

"Not a word of it as argument," replied the preacher. "But, let me ask you, do you believe in a God?"

"I believe in a Power."

"We will not quarrel about the name. Has your Power intelligence?"

"You have my answer."

"Very well. What I call God, you call a Power. It is all the same. Names are nothing. Has your power revealed anything to you?"

"Only in nature—in the rocks, in the forms of matter. And there it stands for all ages, and each one can verify the message to absolute certainty. It has no fables in it. The geologist, like your Moses, can strike upon the rocks, and they will open to him the lesson written upon their imperishable leaves. The language in which their history is embalmed is for all ages and all races, one and the same."

"Indeed!" Do any two of you agree as to what the rocks say? Until lately, during the brief existence of your so-called science, you vehemently said that the earth was formed under a law of uniformity, taking countless ages for the work. Now, we are as confidently told, and as more probable, that the rocks record the results of awful catastrophies, doing in one dreadful minute the changes before supposed to have occupied millenniums of time. According to your views, Nature has been here more millions of years than can be enumerated in our arithmetic, and yet we find her a very coquettish sort of teacher. Nature is silent as to whether we should drink water or wine, eat flesh or vegetables, live in a hot or cool climate, as to what will in all cases cure, and what will in all cases kill, and when we die—

"Ah," says the scientist, "that is the end of us."

"Then you do not believe in the immortality of the soul?"

"Why, no; of course not. What is the difference between the death of a man and the death of a dog? They both rot alike in the earth, and are lost to all knowledge. Why do you think the soul immortal?" continued the skeptic. "You never saw a soul."

"Nor did you ever see an atom," remarked the preacher, "nor gravitation, nor oxygen; and yet you do not doubt their existence."

"But, how can a soul exist without the body?"

"The existence of the soul out of the body is no greater mystery than the existence of the soul in the body."

"It is a sufficient answer to say," replied the skeptic, " that we know of the soul within, but not without the body. We know nothing of the mind without brain-matter."

"Do you know more of the mind with brain-matter? Did mind create matter, or matter create mind?" inquired the preacher.

"I am inclined to admit that mind created matter."

"If mind created matter, then there was a time when mind, in the abstract, was, and matter was not."

"But suppose," remarked the skeptic, "that matter created mind?"

"Then," said the preacher, " matter is competent to continue in eternity what it began in time."

"No doubt," said the skeptic, " that whatever began mind in the past, is competent to carry it on in the future; but will it do it?"

"The law of continuity has brought all things on from the past, and what repeals that law as to the future? Another law, universally and invariably true, is, that to die is gain.

All other things gain by dying ; why should not man ? The soul is self-created, or it is created by another. If self-created, it is a power to itself forever. If it is created by another, then that other can take care of it in the future, as it has in the past. So, whether we exist of ourselves, or by the will of another, there is within and behind us an immortalizing power, looking, to say the least, in the direction of immortality, and showing its possibility."

"But is there a probability of it ?" inquired the skeptic, with an incredulous tone. "When the body dies," he continued, "we see no soul depart, nor has one ever come back to give evidence of its disembodied existence."

"In this, as in everything else," said the preacher, "the past answers for the future. Though no one can have a *present experience*, in the body, of a *future state* out of the body, yet the reasoning from present physical phenomena to future physical phenomena is neither different nor more certain than that from the present existence of the soul to the continued future existence of the soul. The rising of the life-bearing sun to-morrow cannot, in the nature of things, be a matter of observation to-day. In the omnipresence and omnipotence of law, by which both matter and mind continue to progress, we have as much certainty of the continuance of the individual immortality of the soul, as we have of anything in the future. But as you doubt this, the first question to be settled is :

1. Is the Soul of Man Immortal ?

" But, as we have said, we cannot possibly answer experimentally now a question whose solution must be entirely in the future. Do we not live now under a law of persistence, by which it is seen that we must live hereafter ? We exist now, and why should we not continue to exist ? We expect to exist to-morrow, and why should we not expect to exist one hundred or a million of years hence ? In the life of the race, we have not only an expectation and a start in existence, prophetic of its continuance, but really, in our present lives, as conscious individuals of a persistent race, we have already entered upon immortality. We are in the grasp of the law of persistence, and those who deny immortality, must prove conclusively that the law has been repealed and the grasp released. In short, the doctrine of immortality cannot be disproved."

"Nor can it be proved," replied the skeptic. "The individual has no immortality in himself. His race or type only persists."

"And how long do you admit that the race persists?" asked the preacher.

"I admit what I see," replied the skeptic. "We see that nature continues the race or type, but not the individual man."[1]

"Very well," said the preacher, "so far as science can establish a principle of continuity or persistence of beings in time, it helps religion to a line of reasoning, which points to their persistence in eternity. '*We are*, and *therefore shall be.*' You say that the life of both

---

[1] "So careful of the type she seems,
    So careless of the single life."—*Tennyson.*

the race and individuals continues for this world only. We say that life once begun must be supposed to continue, not only in this world, but also in the next, unless it be proved to have ceased. You say that this proof has been made when the material body has no longer life in it. We say that the separation of the soul from the body cannot be a cessation of the existence of the soul, for this separation takes place every second, and yet we live. At no two moments do we have the same bodies, though ever the same souls. As our entire bodies are new every seven years, while our life and consciousness are one and the same, it is evident that we do not give up our consciousness when we give up our bodies, in what we call life, and why should we be held to give it up when we give up our bodies in what we call death?

(*a.*) "*The persistence of the human type or race includes the persistence of the individual.*

"And yet, do you not see that the race goes on, while the individal dies?

"We must closely scrutinize the evidence of

our senses," replied the preacher." "We think we see the sun go round the world, whereas the world actually revolves round the sun. The senses often cheat us, even into superstition. We see nature at work around us; and even if we perfectly understand what she is doing in the present, we cannot be certain of what she will do in the future. We see that decay precedes reproduction; now, may we not, as a conclusion of a long line of analogies, expect death to prelude life? If we, by theology, see as through a glass darkly as to a spiritual future, you have no more light as to nature and its interpretation by science."

"And yet," said the skeptic, "when you attend the funeral of a friend, while the race survives all around, and in you, your own eyes tell you that your friend is dead."

"All that my eyes tell me," replied the preacher, "is that the individual has been changed. We know that the death of a grain of wheat quickens it into a hundred-fold life. We see, but cannot comprehend the transformations of nature. We know no more of the mysterious change that takes man out of the world, than we do of the mystery that brought him into it. The curtain before us is no more impenetrable than the one behind us. In other words, death is no greater mystery than life. If the human race can continue in our sight, why not the individual out of sight? Nature's hidden work is her greatest.

"I do not say what the ultimate value to religion your doctrine of the persistence of race or type may be; but if it proves anything for science, it proves more for religion. Whatever you prove for all, you prove for each. As is the race, so is the individual, and as is the individual, so is the race. Water cannot rise above its level. The chain cannot be stronger than its weakest link. The race cannot transcend the individual. The nature of the ancestor and heir is identical. The race persists by its strength of life, not its weakness of death. Whatever the race has, it must give to the individual ; and whatever the individual receives, it must give back to the race. The race lives by the lives it continues. If the individual is perishable, the race must be perishable; if the race persists, so must the individuals which constitute it. They are in the same ship. Indeed, there is no difference between them. The type is the individual, and the individual is the type. But if there be a difference, there must have been a moment when one was and the other was not. If this were even so, which was first, the type or the individual? If the first man had died before there had been another, would not both type and individual have died? Individual persons make the race, and not the race individuals. As there can be no type or race without individuals, so the persistence of one must be the persistence of the other. Adam was either the race, or only an individual. If he was only an individual, then the individual originated the race. If the individual originated the race, and the race be imperishable, then the individual originated something imperishable. If the individual originated anything imperishable, would not its first care have been to make itself imperishable? Self-persistence was innate in the first man. In other words, was not Adam, while he was the first and only man, in himself both type and individual? And as such, was he not, in your idea, at the same moment both mortal and immortal—mortal as an individual, and immortal as a type? As these conditions were successive, that is, the individual was first and the race or type afterwards, or the reverse, Adam must have either fallen from what you call the immortality of the type to the mortality of the individual, or risen from the mortality of the individual to the immortality of the type. But as it is a law of nature, as you contend, for nature to rise and progress, Adam could not have dropped from immmortality to mortality, but must have risen from mortality to immortality by the upward movement of existence. If Shakespeares and Miltons are evolved from tadpoles and monkeys, as you insist, we find the nature of man taking in more and more of that which must persist, whether it be of type or of the individual. Your Nature-God seems like our God, to keep the best, whatever may be done with the worst. The persistence of the genus includes the persistence of the species. Why should the indefinite type persist and not the definite individual?"

"According to your argument," remarked the skeptic, "you have as many types as you have species or individuals."

"I do not see that," replied the preacher. "The persistence of a principle will illustrate the persistence of a being. The polygon has many sides, and only one figure. To illustrate this, draw an equilateral triangle, and call it No. 1."

"There it is," said the skeptic.

"Now, draw another equilateral triangle, and call it No. 2."

"Very well. Now what?"

"Have you one figure, or two?"

"I have one figure and its copy."

"Not at all. You have two drawings made upon the same principle, entirely irrespective of each other, of one and the same figure. No. 1 is not a pattern to No. 2, nor is No. 2 a copy of No. 1, just as one man is not a copy of another man. They are both originals. That equal sides of a triangle make equal angles is as necessary and independently true in No. 2 as in No. 1, and you might keep on drawing equilateral triangles forever, and each triangle would be an original illustration of the same principle, and make the identical figure. In other words, each individual triangle would be the type, because formed by the same principle; and if the type persists, so does the individual."

"If the triangle be the type, what is the individual?" asked the skeptic.

"The triangle is both type and individual," answered the preacher. "There cannot be any continuity in the type that is not in the individual. The eternal principle upon which one equilateral triangle is formed, is the principle

TYPE AND INDIVIDUAL IDENTICAL. 41

upon which every other equilateral triangle is formed. That which makes a type in one, makes a type wherever that principle is present. That which made Adam or the first man a type, makes every man a type."

"But there is no denying," said the skeptic, "that man, the individual, dies, and yet man, the type, persists."

"If the type, under the principle of essential continuity, persists here, the individual, under the same principle, imparted to or inherited from the type, must persist hereafter. In other words, the individual does not surrender its principle of continuity by change of form or place, any more than the worm ceases to live by metamorphosing itself into a butterfly. The flow of the river is continuous, though some part of its channel may be subterranean."

"I admit," said the skeptic, "that all types persist; but if you use that admission to prove the individual immortality of the human soul through the persistence of the human type, then I insist that the same reasoning proves the individual immortality of the brute soul through the persistence of the brute type. If inextinguishable existence inheres in one persistence, it inheres in all persistences."

"That by no means follows," replied the preacher. "Though types do not mix as would be the case of animals half-born from rocks, or of trees rooted in the backs of animals, and though all living things are half way from something above and something below them, yet things persist according to their nature, one for awhile and another forever. Persistence is not change. It continues and perfects a type through its own era, but it does not lift one type out of itself into another, the material into the spiritual, the unconscious into the conscious, the mortal into the immortal. The spiritual, the conscious, and the immortal must be in the type at its start, or never. Any way, my logic is not invalidated if it prove more than my proposition. Let the brute be immortal! Some brutes would seem to be as fit for immortality as some men. Types persist. That is admitted.

But how about the individual? Is not a chip from the block a part of the block? Is not a drop of ink still ink, though not in the inkstand? Is not a drop of wine from the goblet still wine, though it be only an individual drop? Is not the individual whatever the type is? And has not each type its own duration of persistence? The vegetable type its duration? The animal type its duration? The conscious, spiritual type its duration?"

"As you have so magnified the importance of the persistency of type, of which I made only passing mention," said the skeptic, "let me ask what duration do you ascribe to the persistence of the several types, especially of what you call the conscious, spiritual type?"

"As the conscious, spiritual type," said the preacher, "is at the summit of things, I suppose it will persist as long as things have a summit. I can conceive of no reason for a change. But any way, that is a question for you to answer. As you proposed the doctrine of persistence, it is for you to show where persistence ends.

Matter persists forever. Energy persists forever; and if we apply Mr. Herbert Spencer's test of truth, the inconceivability of the opposite, we must admit that, as consciousness possesses an independent existence of its own, at the summit of everything, it, too, must persist forever.[1] For my part, I do not know what this law of persistence is, which may extend from a second through an eternity, only that it is. Do you know any more of it? What is this law of life? Who knows? Do you?

"I see things go on continuously, 'the herb yielding seed after his kind, and the tree yielding fruit, whose seed is in itself, after his kind.' I do not know, from any light of science, how things began, nor how they continue. I do not know what oxygen is, or what electricity is, or what force is. Do you? I do not know what matter is, or what mind is. Do you? In short, who knows what anything is? Do you? But, although science does not inform me what the

---

[1] Eccles, Popular Science Monthly, July, 1878, p. 356. Butler's Analogy, Chap. I.

LAW DEFINED.

law of persistence is, or any other law, my own opinion is that all law is will."

" Whose will ? "

" You ask Schœpenhaur and Tyndal, and I will ask David and Paul. One thing is certain, laws do not make themselves. If there be any such thing as laws, which some of you skeptics now doubt, we know, from the unity of the economy of the world, that there is but one Law-giver."

" If you can prove, as a trick of words, that the man is the race, and the race is the man," said the skeptic, " each man is conscious that he is his own individual self, and not the race. I know that my mind is my own, and I know that it is not yours. Each man's consciousness assures him of the ridiculousness of your whole argument."

" Then you believe in the testimony of consciousness," said the preacher.

" I would be a fool if I did not," said the skeptic.

" Then," said the preacher, " I contend that

(*b.*) "*The persistence of consciousness proves the immortality of the soul.*"

"Are you crazy," asked the skeptic, "or are you trifling with my common sense?"

"Neither," answered the preacher. "Common sense is so rare that I would not trifle with it under any circumstances, more especially with you, in this conversation. It is the ground upon which I claim to be, and where I should be glad to find you. Each one is conscious, as you say, that his mind is his own, and continuous. Each one has the same reason to believe in the individuality and continuous personality of his own mind, that he has to believe in its existence. And we may as well expect the mind itself to perish, as to expect its individuality and personal continuance to perish. We know that we know; in other words, we are conscious, and therefore immortal."[1]

---

[1] "The exercises of the mind arise and vanish, and are each separate and distinct from others in their appearance; but the same mind is in and through them all, and holds them all in its one consciousness. The thought which was yesterday or last year in consciousness, and the conscious thought of

"Consciousness persists because, first, it is immaterial, uncompounded, and, therefore, indissoluble ; and second, because it is at the summit of beings, and survives as the fittest. Consciousness is either inherent in matter, or it is an independent attribute. If it inheres in matter, it inheres in each and every atom, or in a combination of atoms. If it inheres in a com-

to-day are both recognized as being in the same self-consciousness. The self-consciousness has not changed, while the exercises have been coming and departing. The mind thus remains in its own identity yesterday and onward into the future, perpetuating the same mind. Through all development of its faculties, in all states, the mind itself neither comes nor goes, but retains its self-sameness through all changes. Its phenomenal experience varies *in* time, but itself perdures *through* all time." (Hickok, Science of the Mind from Consciousness, Chap. I, p. 3.)

"Consciousness has been very differently apprehended by different writers, and certainly not seldom misapprehended. Some have considered it as scarcely to be distinguished from personal identity ; others as a separate faculty for knowing the action of all other mental powers ; and others again as the complement and connection of all mental exercises, inasmuch as they are all held in one consciousness. Consciousness is doubtless ever one in the same person, otherwise some actions would be in one consciousness, and some in another, and man's life could never be brought into one experience. But this does by no means confound consciousness in personal identity, for identity continues in and through a great number of states of consciousness." (Ibid. 88.)

bination of atoms, then it must inhere in each atom; for, as nothing can communicate what it has not, each atom must have inherently in itself the consciousness which it communicates to a combination of atoms. As consciousness is personality, if each atom is conscious, each man is not one person, but as many persons as there are atoms in his body. But as our bodies are no two seconds the same, if each atom is conscious, and, therefore, a person, we are not only a congress, but an endless procession of persons, which is inconceivable. The nature of every cause must include its effects; but, as we cannot conceive of anything being and not being at the same moment, so the nature of unconsciousness cannot include consciousness, and unconsciousness cannot, therefore, be the cause of consciousness as an effect. If consciousness be indivisible, it cannot be an inherent energy in divisible matter.

"Consciousness can become extinct in only one of three ways: either, first, by *dissolution*, which is impossible, as consciousness is a single, not a compound substance, and cannot be dissolved ; or, second, by *privation* of a part of its essence ; but as consciousness has no parts, it can be deprived of none ; or, third, by *annihilation;* but this could only be by its own act, which is not supposable, unless by the external act of God, whose existence you deny."

"But," said the skeptic, "it can be annihilated by the God whose existence you preachers admit."

"Our God says that our spirits shall return to Him who gave them. But let us keep to the skeptical line of argument, for it is this I wish to meet.

"As a principle of unity, the soul is indiscerptible and indestructible ; as a principle of motion, it is incapable of rest ; as a vital principle, it is incapable of annihilation ; as a self-conscious principle, it is incapable of oblivion."[1]

"Why is personal consciousness *therefore* immortal, as you remarked a moment since ? " asked the skeptic.

[1] Heard's Tripartite Nature of Man, p. 3.

"The immortality of the soul," replied the preacher, "is not impossible from any connection with matter, for it is not matter. As nature can make no leaps, unconscious matter could never have become conscious matter. That matter should think is unthinkable. The body changes constantly, but never the consciousness. Each persists or not by its own laws. Herbert Spencer says that there is no conceivable kind of consciousness which does not imply continued existence as its datum.[1] Nature confines life in unconsciousness below. Supernature enlarges it in consciousness above."

"Or rather," remarked the skeptic, "first prove that the soul or consciousness of man is anything but an effect, and anything more to the body than music is to the instrument; that it is a reality and not a mere name."

---

[1] First Prin., chap. VI, sec. 62. After the text was written, the Popular Science Monthly for July, 1878, brought me a most admirable article, by R. G. Eccles, Esq., on the "Radical Fallacy of Materialism," wherein he says, at the conclusion of a line of most convincing argument: "If we declare matter and energy to be eternal, then we must declare the same of consciousness." p. 360.

"Let us not," replied the preacher, "plunge into the old discussion of the school-men, as to the distinction between nominalism and realism. If consciousness or the soul itself be an effect, then it persists; for all effects not only succeed, but survive their causes. The soul or mind is something, or it is nothing. If it be nothing, then as nothing, it cannot be destroyed. If it can be destroyed, then it must be something, for destruction implies something to be destroyed. But if it be something, it cannot be destroyed; for while nature changes all things that are changeable, she destroys nothing that she values as anything."

"Nature," said the skeptic, "may preserve the soul as a part of the general force of the universe, and yet destroy its consciousness, and so its personality; in other words, reabsorb it, as the Buddhists believe."

"Then she destroys the soul itself," replied the preacher; "for the soul to be a soul must retain its individual and conscious personality. But in any view you may take, immortality is sure. We see the proof of it in this, among other considerations: Consciousness makes a person and distinguishes man in the scale of being, whether he be an original type or a derived individual; whether he be the fountain or the issuing stream. If man derives this being, it must be from some conscious cause. If he originates his own consciousness, he creates it as a God, and he can continuously transmit it as a God. In his consciousness, man shows that he is either descended by creation from some conscious God, or that, in consciousness, he is himself a God to his conscious descendants. Therefore, whether he begins in a God as a source of conscious being, or a God begins in him as a source of conscious being, he is immortal, for nothing divine ever dies."

"What fallacies, I might say sophistries," remarked the skeptic.

"Why so?" inquired the other.

"Do you not apply physical principles to psychological conditions?" asked the skeptic.

"Is the logic of matter not the same as the logic of mind?"

"We know nothing about the mind," answered the skeptic.

"Do you know anything more about matter?" replied the preacher.[1]

[1] "Six hundred years before Christ, Thales taught that all things sprung from water ; Anaximines was as certain that all things were made out of air ; Pythagoras held to the inexplicable theory of numbers as the source of all matter ; Xenophanes believed and insisted that all things were but parts of one Pleroma or Being ; Parmenides said that all things came from one great thought ; Zeno held to a pantheistic Godhead ; Empedocles was certain that four elements originated all things ; Democritus conceived the idea that all nature came from eternal atoms ; Heroclitus had a theory of fire and motion ; Anaxagoras held the truth of a world-forming intelligence. What beautiful confusions !

"If science be an indisputable authority, its progressive utterances must be uniform and universal. But this is notoriously not the case. Buckle says that moral truth is unchangeable, but that of the intellect not so. This is fortunate for moral truth and the moral certainty of the world, but most unfortunate for the claim of mere intellectual progress to direct conduct and the world. History gives us but little certainty as to how science will change its conclusions. First, it may be from error to error, as from the erroneous theory of Hipparchus to the no less errors of Ptolemy ; second, it may be from error to truth, as from the errors of the Pagan Ptolemy to the divine truth of the Christian Copernicus ; third, it may be from truth to error, as from the teachings of Copernicus to those of his successor and pupil, Tycho Brahe ; fourth, it may be from one divine truth to another divine truth, as from the teachings of Copernicus to those of Newton. Varro says three hundred different philosophers held as many different opinions concerning the Deity, and two hundred and eighty

"You have," said the skeptic, "the most unfair way of putting things."

"Do the skeptics," inquired the preacher, "put things in any fairer way ? Like the pagan priests, who have ceased to believe what they preached, no two speculative scientists, who know how they have entertained the intelligence of the age with conjectured facts and radical inferences, can look each other in the face without laughing. They use special and sounding words, as if these represented established truth instead of novel theories, and they capture the credulity of the ignorant by the confidence of their assumptions. They do a very big business on exceedingly small capital. They talk of atoms, molecules, conservation of force, and protoplasms, as if they were the most certain of things. Except as to pure and applied mathematics, and the science of the practical arts, what one of your theories is established ? From the confident air with which you advance them, the unlearned think them

of these held divers opinions concerning the supreme good or ground of morality."

all to be true, as you state them. You destroy the faith of the young, and offer nothing to the old but the grinning skeleton of knowledge. You use words as if they were proofs and arguments.[1]

"You sneer at the scientific learning of the clergy, as if the great secrets of nature lay hid in the crucible and retort of the materialists alone, or would reveal themselves only to the scalpel of you skeptics. The pages of nature are open alike to all, and all educated men are men of science. The black arts of the chemists no longer alarm. There is no hierarchy to the knowledge of nature. You know what others know, and no more. Your opinions respecting physical phenomena are of no more value than those of any other diligent student, clerical or lay. You sneer with a contemptuous intolerance at all who do not concur in your assertions to-day, and yet to-morrow you are made to swallow your own pulverized theories.

[1] Prof. Emil Du Bois Raymond says : "Modern natural science, parodoxical as the statement is, owes its origin to Christianity." Popular Science Monthly, July, 1878.

A scientific bigot is arrogant with a special knowledge and a general ignorance. Your own Vinchow says: 'Of all kinds of dogmatism, the materialistic is the most dangerous, because it denies its own dogmatism, and appears in the garb of science ; because it professes to rest on fact, when it is but speculation; and because it attempts to annex territories to natural science, before they have been fairly conquered.' "[1]

"I will not resent the discourtesy of these remarks," said the skeptic. "You clergy are impatient of contradiction, and tremble lest the light of science should dissipate the darkness of religious credulity. The priest sees his altar deserted and himself without followers. Theological studies narrow the mind and spoil the temper."

"If we theologians who study most the existence of an infinite God be narrow-minded, what must be the narrow-mindedness of you scientists who study only the existence of a finite and imaginary atom ?

"Excuse me, if I spoke too earnestly, and

[1] Nature, Nov. 1874.

let us keep in good humor with each other, for neither of us know any too much."

"That's true," admitted the skeptic, good-naturedly.

"But," said the preacher, "do not fancy that we are on the same level; for while we *believe* much, there is so much that you do *not* know. Whatever our speculative errors may be, they most certainly mould character, improve institutions, and help conduct; but your speculative errors break down all hope, and build up nothing but despair. Taking your theories at what you claim for them, let me ask you, Does nature change by receding or advancing? Does she ever tear down anything except to build up something better? When she decomposes vegetable life, is it not to build up animal life? If our consciousness be destroyed, must it not be for some condition above consciousness? What do you *know* of the origin of life? of organization? of the connection between matter and mind? What you *do* know is limited, but what you do *not* know is unlimited.[1] Does matter mentalize itself, or mind materialize itself ? You evolutionists have never answered the question whether the egg preceded and was adapted to the chicken, or the chicken to the egg ; whether the male was made before and for the female, or the female before and for the male; whether the honey was made for the bee or the bee for the honey. The Unknown is vast indeed ! Do not all things advance ? ''

" Advance would seem to be," admitted the skeptic, " in accordance with a law of nature in the past, certainly."

" Then you must prove that it has been repealed as to the future."

" But," replied the skeptic, "if nature tears down the vegetables on one plane to build up the animals on a higher plane, why should not the brute develope into something above itself ? If man can become an angel, why not the brute

---

[1] See Dr. Montgomery's "Monera, or the Problem of Life," Pop. Science Monthly, August, 1878; Supplement Pop. S. M., May, 1878, Virchow, 12, 73 ; also, July number, p. 334; Tyndall, Address, Norwich, 1868.

become a man ? If, as according to the analogy of nature, conscious man is to be lifted into some power above consciousness, ought not the unconscious brute to be lifted above itself into consciousness ? I insist, that if development is to be expected in men, so it ought to be in brutes."

"We can look below us and see that no brute ever does become a man ; but we cannot look above us in the same way to see what a man may expect to become," replied the preacher. "Immortality is necessarily to be expected from nature in either man or brutes, or both, unless she can be stupid enough to stop in sight of what would glorify her most. If she can produce life for awhile in man and brute, why not life forever ? Has not nature as much reason to go on as she had to begin ? And since beginning, has she not in fact steadily advanced, and held every gain ? As to thinking animals, no intelligence short of consciousness is considered a gain."

" Are not brutes conscious ? "

"We have no knowledge that they are. Whatever mind the brutes may have, so far as we now know, seems limited to their animal wants. It is directive, not reflective.[1] But man has mind for far more. Brute mind is imperishable, only as an impersonal, unconscious mode of force, in the same grade of force it is now; but lacking consciousness, it is perishable as mind. The mind-force of man persists in its consciousness. It is consciousness which lifts mind from a mode or manifestation of force into force itself. Conscious mind is force."

"In distinguishing between individuality and personality, do you not make a distinction without a difference?"

"Not at all. Consciousness is the grand difference between individuality and personality, and is a new order of existence. Nature preserves its best things, and these only. If it preserves not consciousness, what else would it preserve?

[1] Gould's Origin of Religious Ideas, p. 51.

BRUTES NOT PERSONS. 61

" When brutes die, the intelligent but unconscious force that was individualized in them for a time obeys the law of all unconscious, unpersonalized force, and losing whatever individuality it may have exhibited when it has performed any special work, is correlated back into something else, or reabsorbed : as, after electricity has been captured and made to fire guns, ring bells, explode mines, and carry messages across vast oceans and broad continents, it drops its temporary mode of individuality, and, lapsing back like a wave of the sea, becomes again an undistinguishable part of electricity elsewhere, or is correlated into heat. Individuality was no part of its nature, but only an impersonal, unconscious manifestation of it. So the individualized mind of the brute, not having gained consciousness, or enough to lift it into the higher order of personalized force, drops its individuality when its animal work is done, as a tree or an oyster drops its individuality; and being only unconscious force, is conservated, like any other unconscious force, by correlation or reabsorption. But the personality of man, including the individuality common to the brute, and also a consciousness which is peculiar to man, is a vast flight upward; and manifests, if it does not originate, as before said, a new order of force in which individuality, now lifted into personality, persists. Consciousness, or life, on nature's highest terrace, is a gain to be conservated, if any is to be conservated. To individuality there has been superadded, in conscious intelligence, moral power and spiritual responsibility, all that is meant by personality. Nature advances as much in moving from unconsciousness to consciousness, as she does when the animal kingdom rises above the vegetable kingdom. Is there a greater difference between these kingdoms than there is between conscious man thinking about his thought, and the unconscious brute thinking only about his mate and his food? If the law of progress be admitted, then immortality begins where consciousness begins, and ends where it ends. Disembodied life is not new in the nature of things, if mind preceded matter. Conscious mind is either a mode of matter, or it is above matter. If above, it can survive in the future, as in the past, the absence of that which is beneath it. If mind be a mode of matter, it must be a supreme mode, conscious, individual, and personal; and as such, it must exist forever, because no matter perishes. If, in other words, matter becomes a person, then as personalized matter it is perishable. If matter becomes conscious, then it must exist as conscious matter."

"I would like to get your idea of the distinction between individuality and personality, already alluded to, more clearly," remarked the skeptic.

"Then," said the preacher, "every person is an individual, but every individual is not a person. We cannot transcend our personality. A person is an individual that is conscious of his individuality—a thinker conscious of his thought—one who knows that he knows.

A stone or a piece of metal is an individual mass or lump which may be separated into parts, each of which shall continue to have the same qualities as the whole. That which cannot be parted into several things of the same nature is an individual whole; as, for instance, a seed, a plant or an animal, when separated into parts, loses its identity or individuality, which is not retained by any of its parts. We refuse *personality* to a stone or a metal, because these things exist for others and not for themselves. We refuse it also to a mere animal, because, though it may have individuality, it is not conscious of its individuality. We ascribe personality to man because that which he is, he is for himself, and has consciousness of it. Consciousness, or the ability to study our own minds, pre-eminently distinguishes man from the brute—the person from the individual. It is the dividing line between imperishable personality and perishable individuality. Until personality is attained, there is no such individuality as needs or does persist. Though consciousness is not in itself a force, yet, when force becomes conscious, consciousness persists with the persistence of the force that manifests it."

"Men die!" continued the skeptic.

"Yes," answered the preacher, "the individual or unconscious animal part dies, but not the conscious or personal part."

"Why does the unconscious die and not the conscious?"

"Because," replied the preacher, "the animal begets the animal and it dies; God gives the conscious part from himself, and it lives on. We can conceive of no consciousness that does not continue.[1] To resolve personal consciousness back into impersonal consciousness is not to correlate or transform, but to destroy it, and nature destroys nothing."

"Does not nature destroy the individuality of the brute at its death?" inquired the skeptic.

"She drops it," replied the preacher, "but

---

[1] Herbert Spencer's Opinion, *ante*, p. 12.

she seems not to consider the obliteration of any individuality short of conscious individuality, rising into personality, as a destruction or loss. Consciousness is at the summit of all things, and it is consciousness that makes individuality a type, and so a gain. Personality is equal to a type, but if personal consciousness does not persist, then it is a total loss, and nature works in vain, preserving her lower, impersonal types, and annihilating her highest personal, conscious individuals. Such an exhibition of power, such vacillating weakness of purpose, and such permission of loss, if not wanton destruction, would proclaim nature to be an idiot and a suicide. She may convert impersonal and unconscious force, and exalt conscious force, but not destroy it. The elements of everything that dies can be and are used over again, such as the carbon and other elements in the animal body; but that which cannot be used over again does not die. The consciousness of one cannot be used again in the consciousness of another, and unless each man's consciousness persists under all changes, then consciousness, which is the most exalted of facts, must perish altogether. Does nature in anything else so destroy its best work? It is in consciousness that man is in the likeness of God, or whatever is supreme above him. In the pyramid of cannon balls all serve and glorify the one at the top; as in the universe, consciousness looks down upon all unconscious forms below it. Is it in the way of nature that the top alone shall perish, and all below it persist?"

"Brutes are not immortal, because, while they have individuality they have not consciousness, or anything that nature cares to preserve, except their material elements. Having no conscious personality, they must forever remain in the class of impersonal things, and be correlated or transmitted from one impersonal thing to another. Below personal individuality, no individuality persists."

"Nothing persists," said the skeptic, "but type, matter, and force."

"Very well, then," continued the preacher, "as we have considered the immortality of man from the persistence of type, the continuity of consciousness, and not pausing now to consider how far the imperishableness of matter might prove the imperishableness of the soul, I will show that :

(*c.*) *The persistence or conservation of force proves the immortality of the soul.*

"I open and shut my hand. What does that?"

"Mind," answered the skeptic.

"Is that mind which opens and shuts the muscles of the hand the same thing as the muscles?"

"No," said the scientist, with a shrug; "I suppose it might be called a force."

"What is force?"

"Anything that moves matter."

"Then if I understand you, mind is force, because it moves matter?"

"Yes."

"Again : I hold the bulb of this thermometer in my hand, and the mercury rises. What makes it rise ?" asked the preacher.

"The heat of your body," was the answer.

"Is the heat of my body a force, too," asked the preacher.

"Yes," was the reply.

"What is the difference," asked the preacher, "between the mind-force, which opens and shuts my hand, and the heat or matter-force, which makes the mercury rise in the thermometer?"

"Mind-force thinks and matter-force does not," answered the skeptic.

"What do you mean," said the skeptic, "by mind-force ?"

"You scientists," replied the preacher, "say that whatever moves matter is a force. I call mind a force because it moves matter, and whatever you predicate of force you can predicate of mind."

"Hold on a moment," interrupted the skeptic. "Prove to me that mind moves matter."

"By what power," asked the preacher, "do you crook your finger?"

"By the power of my will."

"Is not the will, then, a force?"

"No. It is only the manifestation of a force."

"Is not the will the force," asked the preacher, "and the crooking of the finger the manifestation? If the will is not a force in itself, but only a manifestation, of what force is it a manifestation? Of the mind?"

"No," replied the skeptic. "The mind itself, like all else, is only the manifestation of what Herbert Spencer calls Absolute Force, The Unknown Cause, The Unconditioned Reality."

"Then," replied the preacher, "the act of crooking your finger is the manifestation of your will as a sort of force, and your will the manifestation of your mind as a sort of force behind the will, and your mind the manifestation of the absolute force. In other words, the act of crooking your finger is the manifestation of a manifestation of a manifestation of the absolute force or the unknown cause. Clear, is it not? Either change your definition of force, or admit, fairly and squarely, that mind is a force; and if a force, as imperishable as all other force. Your confusion is, in making all force only manifestations of the one absolute force; which squints at Pantheism. It seems clear that force, and its manifestations, are two things. For instance, heat or will-power moves a body. Now, it is evident that the *motion* is the *manifestation*, and heat, or the will, is the force. In this sense, Herbert Spencer is right; the motion or manifestation disappears, while the force behind it persists."

"Still," asked the skeptic, "do you not in the doctrine of the immortality of the soul, as conservated mind-force, prove too much?"

"How so?"

"Do you not prove the immortality of the souls of brutes? They think, their minds move matter, and are therefore a force; if a force, their minds must be imperishable, if for that reason human minds are."

"I should not regret it if they were, but the immortality of brute-minds would not disprove the immortality of human minds. The soul of man has a personal immortality in having consciousness, for the want of which the mind of the brute is mortal."

"Prove that."

"I think, and I think about my thought; in other words, I am conscious."

"Yes."

"Does the brute think about its thought? Is it conscious?"

"Of course not—or, at least, we have no evidence that it is."

"Then conscious mind-force belongs exclusively to man, making him a *person;* and unconscious mind-force belongs exclusively to brutes, leaving them in the class of thinking but unconscious *things.*"

"Yes."

"We have seen that each man has in himself two orders of force: a conscious, personalizing, regulative mind-force, as seen in his will, elevating him into a person; and an unconscious, impersonal, regulated matter-force, as seen in the heat of his material body, which he has in common with mere things. The brute has the same two orders of force, but its mind-force is as unconscious as its matter-force. Its intelligence is called instinct, and only directive, not reflective, and is limited, unconscious, impersonal, and without moral responsibility."

"Admitted."

"I asked you before, whence did force come, and whither did it go?"

"And I answered that force was and is, and that force ever will be."

"You admitted that force was, therefore, imperishable."

"Yes."

"Then why not the mind of man?"

"It is imperishable, and so, I still contend, is the mind of the brute; but at death all mind, whether of man or of the brute, becomes as impersonal and unconscious as gravitation."

"Not quite so fast, if you please. How do you know that you have a mind at all?"

"I am conscious of it."

"You admitted," said the preacher, "that the brute was not conscious of his mind."

"Yes."

"Here, then, there is at once a wide and unbridged gulf between man and the brute."

"If," said the skeptic, "mind as a force immortalizes man as a conscious person, why should it not immortalize a mere brute as an unconscious individual? Force is force."

"But all force is not the same force. To our observation there are two orders: first, a mind-force, underived and supreme in the Unoriginated Power—personal, intelligent, conscious, and dominating all below it; and second, matter-force, such as heat and gravitation, impersonal, unconscious, unintelligent and secondary to all force above it. You scientists say now that there is but one force in all the universe, conscious in mind and unconscious in matter. Though you do not prove this unity of force, yet, admitting it to be so as the last conclusion of science and for the sake of the argument, even then the unconscious, such as heat and electricity, must be a mode of the conscious, having its basis, as Herbert Spencer says, in Absolute Being, and not the conscious its basis in the unconscious. Even if all force is but eternal power in action, conscious in mind, unconscious in matter, it must ever go forward, but never backward. So that if matter-force cannot be annihilated, neither, *a fortiori*, can mind-force, of which matter-force is the unconscious, impersonal mode. To make the whole reasoning plain beyond a doubt, challenging the detection of a fallacy, I will state it in the argument of two syllogisms, which you must admit or deny:

"Whatever moves matter is a force. Mind moves matter; therefore mind is a force."

The skeptic was silent.

The preacher continued: "All force is imperishable. The mind is a force; therefore all mind is imperishable."

"Ah!" interposed the skeptic, "I deny the major premise of this last syllogism; you must prove that *all* force is imperishable."

"How do you prove that *any* force is imperishable?" replied the preacher.

"I prove the imperishableness of any and of all force," replied the skeptic, "by the admitted fact that its quantity is fixed ; that is, that force can be neither increased nor diminished, neither created nor destroyed. Do you not believe this ?"

"I do not admit conservation of force to be the fact, in your terms," replied the preacher, "but only that such is the theory by which you scientists try to account for phenomena that can, as yet, be accounted for as well in no other way."

"You certainly do not tell me," exclaimed the skeptic, "that you, with your learning, do not accept the doctrine of the conservation and correllation of force ?"

"I accept it as much as Herbert Spencer accepts it.

'Fools rush in where angels fear to tread.'

Those who know the most say the least. Herbert Spencer says[1] 'the persistence of force is an ultimate truth of which no inductive proof is possible.' Youmans says 'it is not without its difficulties, which time alone must be trusted to remove.'[2] Grove, Faraday, Stewart, LeConte and Bain assume, rather than attempt to prove, the doctrine of the conservation of force. Do *you* believe these doctrines yourself? I can see such correllation as heat into electricity, and of electricity into heat; but I do not see gravitation correllated or transferred into any other manifestation of force, or of any other force into gravitation. Besides, if force can be and is exhaustively correllated backwards and forwards, how can your theory of evolution be true, that everything progresses forever? The constancy or inconstancy in the quantity of force depends upon whether its source is personal or impersonal, and this ques-

[1] First Principles, Chap. VI, § 59.
[2] Introduction to Cor. and Con. of Forces, xiv.

tion of source must be first settled. The manifestation of impersonal force, that is, force manifested in things as well as persons—such as the blind force of heat, electricity, or gravitation—is as an ocean of force lifted and broken at times into individual waves that lapse and subside into the infinite fullness. Personal or will force, originating in the mind of an Infinite Person, is deposited and perpetually correllated in the wills of finite, conscious persons. If a Person did not create force, force has certainly created not only a person, but multitudes of persons, for man is here. If there be no God, and unintelligent, eternal Force created everything, then it was indeed a miraculous leap for the conscious force manifested in every man's will to come up out of what you call unconscious force lurking only in matter. If unconscious force originated everything, which one of its forces did the work? Did unconscious gravitation create everything? Did unconscious electricity create everything? Did unconscious chemical affinity create everything?

"Do you deny that the quantity of force in the universe is fixed?" inquired the skeptic.

"Why should it be fixed, and who is to fix it?" replied the preacher.

"Excuse me, if I insist upon a direct answer."

"Then," said the preacher, "I admit that the quantity of force is fixed; but it is *infinite*."

"Nonsense!" exclaimed the skeptic.

"It is more logical, and not so difficult," replied the preacher, to suppose that your creative nature, in originating and fixing the quantity of force would have provided an infinite quantity, than to suppose that she would have experimented upon the possible insufficiency of a finite quantity."

"How could there be any 'possible insufficiency' of force, even if the quantity were finite?" asked the skeptic, in a puzzled tone.

"If nature had any plan to which she invariably worked, we might suppose that she would have known exactly how much and what kind of force she would need, and might, with good reason, have fixed its quantity in finite limits;

but as you, Buckner, Vogt, and Moleschott, deny that there is design or plan in nature, she could not, therefore, know how much force she might need in her blind work, and might well be expected to fix enough once for all, and make it infinite. Any way, nature, in the prodigality of her works, seems to be quite confident of having enough stuff to keep up, and even extend, her phenomena. The quantity of force must be infinite or self-limited; for you deny any God to limit it. But if you say that it is not infinite, then you must prove definitely how much less it is; because if it be not infinite it may be zero, and vanish entirely. I admit that force is in the universe. Those who assert a given quantity must define and prove the quantity. The fact is, my unbelieving friend, neither you nor any one else knows much about this thing you call force. The definition of force I have used is about as good as any, if not the best; but keep in mind that I argue this question from your exclusive standpoint of science, not from mine, of both science and revelation. "But to return to the source of force : to what source do you attribute it?"

"Of course," answered the skeptic, "to an impersonal one."

"Then you differ from Spencer and Wallace, on this point. Herbert Spencer says : 'The axiomatic truths of physical science unavoidably postulate Absolute Being as their common basis. We cannot construct a theory of internal phenomena without postulating Absolute Being ; and unless we postulate Absolute Being, or Being which persists, we cannot construct a theory of external phenomena. Thus there is even a more profound agreement between Religion and Science than was before shown.'[1]

"Wallace, on Natural Selection, says : 'If, therefore, we have traced one force, however minute, to an origin in our own WILL, while we have no knowledge of any other primary cause of force, it does not seem an improbable conclusion that all force may be *will*-force; and thus, that the whole universe is not merely de-

[1] First Principles, Chap. IX, § 60.

pendent on, but actually *is*, the WILL of higher intelligences, or of one Supreme Intelligence.'[1]

"So far as these authorities can settle it, force has its basis in Absolute Being. If this be so, the quantity of force is not necessarily fixed, but may vary with the decisions of His omnific will, and so transcend the domain and methods of science."

"I respectfully differ," in this matter, said the skeptic, "from both of these eminent philosophers. As you say, to admit that force has its basis in the will, is necessarily to admit that its quantity may possibly be inconstant, and its investigation altogether outside of scientific methods."

"What then," inquired the preacher, "is the source of force, and how do you account for what you see around us?"

"I cannot account for anything. Things are here, and that is all we know about them," was the reply.

---

[1] Natural Selection, p. 368. See Monera, August No. Popular Science Monthly, 457.

"For what end were they designed?" asked the preacher.

"For no design," was the answer. "Things are just as they are, and we should not have found them less full of design had they been different. The forces act necessarily blindly."

"Of course, if you know nothing, you can say nothing as to the origin of things; but how do they act?"

"Their activity is from an immanent, necessary instinct."

"I suppose," remarked the preacher, "that, as Büchner says, I ought to understand what it means, but I do not. What does it mean?"

"If we have time, I will come back to this question with pleasure," said the skeptic.

"Very well," replied the preacher. "Is this instinct intelligent, conscious, and eternal? Explain to me this Impersonal Nature that is to your system what a Personal God is to mine."

"Then," said the skeptic, "let us suppose that, originally, there was a given quantity of force as raw material—one mass—blind, impersonal, unconscious, incoherent, never to be increased or diminished; and under what law, as we study the nature of Nature, would it be seen instantly to act? Necessarily, under the law of self-variation, first into minerals, then into vegetables, then into animals, and finally, as we see the fact to be, into conscious personality. Nothing keeps still. Like a stick stood for a second on end, but must fall, everything is in unstable equilibrium. Herbert Spencer, having announced that the integration of matter and the dissipation of motion was the law of evolution, following Von Baer in this one thought, proclaimed that the doctrine of THE INSTABILITY OF THE HOMOGENEOUS IS THE FIRST SUBORDINATE LAW OF EVOLUTION. All matter is restless, and in a state of perpetual motion. Absolutely nothing is at rest; atoms, molecules, masses, society, nations—everything is unstable. Conceive that to be a law, and we catch an idea how phenomena arose. From the result, that THE MULIPLICATION OF EFFECTS IS THE

SECOND SUBORDINATE LAW OF EVOLUTION, everything moves, and therefore, everything changes. In other words, *all sameness tends to variety.* In the Spencerian phrase, the homogeneous becomes the heterogeneous. Nature abhors monotony, sameness, universal centripetalism. The sun is one, but its beams are many. A ray of light again is itself dissolved by everything on which it falls. The crocus consumes its red and blue, and rejects its yellow. The leaf consumes its red, and rejects its blue and yellow after mixing them into green. The geranium will distribute on one of its leaves, as on the palette of the artist, every scale and tone, and every imaginable hue and tint of color. Stones and woods and fruits paint themselves unlike; and on sky and sea and earth, as on the proscenium of the universe, the pencil of light varies every line, and glorifies all with a perpetual newness."

" You interest me very much ! "

" So, too," continued the scientist, " in a mass of assimilating food, one element betakes itself to the bones, another to the tissues, and another to the nerves. In the mind, one power is in thought, another in feeling, and another in action. In motion, one seeks the center, and another flies off from the center. In leafage, how opposed is the unfolding! Groups balance groups, and mass balances mass; and from the one system of roots, and the one trunk, how unity expands itself into variety; and the homogeneous becomes the heterogeneous!"

"You might say that this necessary instinct is a creative instinct," interrupted the preacher.

"But this is not all," continued the other. "We are now prepared to announce that SEGREGATION IS THE THIRD SUBORDINATE LAW OF EVOLUTION. In other words: *All unity tends to plurality.* The one makes itself many. Attraction and repulsion are universal antitheses. Individuality is omnipresent phenomena. Succession is difference. There are no two things alike in all the universe—no two atoms, no two sounds, no two colors, no two lines or forms come from the same mould. Nature is a creator, not a mechanic. Though nature, with all her originality, may seem to imitate her own works, she is too affluent absolutely to repeat them. Though nature has but one force, she behaves as if she had several, so anxious is she to divide herself. For a long time scientists thought and talked of heat, electricity, gravitation, and chemical affinity as different forces. But whether nature really divides up the totality of force in this way or not, she never intermits her movement from oneness to unity, from sameness to variety; grading every line, form, sound, and color in the universe. From the mass she advanced to different worlds; then into ascending kingdoms of minerals; then to genera, and species of vegetables and animals; then to individuals, with such minute variation as to forbid repetition, and to preclude identity everywhere and in everything; and then she advanced to conscious personality. And yet there was no increase in the quantity of force; certainly, no diminution. If there was change, there was no loss."

"Would not the birth of a soul, as it is a separate unit of force, disturb the equilibrium of force?" asked the preacher.

"Not at all," answered the skeptic. "Suppose every soul born into the world to be a part of the totality of this unconscious, impersonal force, the ever-increasing number of souls does not increase the quantity of force in the universe, even if they never return to their original fountain. A thing may change its manifestations by correlation, without increasing or decreasing its essence. Correlation neither creates nor destroys. The quantity of force is not affected when heat is transformed into electricity, or electricity into heat. A pound of molten lead is still a pound, whether it be molded into individual bullets or remains in the molten mass. So, a portion of unconscious, impersonal force, or the whole of it, may be changed for all time to come into personal force, in the units of human souls, without disturbing the assumed constancy of its original quantity. The subtrahend and remainder equal the minuend. What unconscious, persistent impersonality loses, conscious personality gains, and persistent correlation does not disturb the equilibrium. And as the tendency of things is from sameness to variety, and from one to many, from the inorganic to the organic, from the indefinite to the definite, from the unconscious to the conscious, there is every reason, in this habit of nature, to expect the impersonal, unconscious mass to correlate and perpetuate itself in the units of conscious, personal individuality."

"It seems to me that you are getting on my ground. Be careful about your admissions," continued the preacher, "for I shall use all these principles which you are laying down so clearly against your side."

"You are welcome to all the comfort or support you get out of my admissions," replied the skeptic.

"It may not be much," rejoined the preacher, "but I shall make the most of them. You have shown how this 'necessary instinct' makes things differ; but how does it hold on to things, or make things hold on to it?"

"Of course you do not concur with me in opinion," remarked the skeptic.

"I do not differ from you more than you do from me," said the preacher.

"Nevertheless," continued the skeptic, "*all real advances persist.* Nature never recalls or intermits progression; never mistakes the end or the means; never changes in vain; never sees a reason to undo what she has once done; never goes down, but always upward and forward."

"So much for phenomena from impersonal nature! And yet," remarked the preacher, "there is no talk of a true explanation. The mind, accustomed to abstraction, is the dupe of an illusion when it takes laws for realities. Laws are symbols of order; they do not account for order.[1] We are told that as the motion which is in everything dissipates, matter integrates. That is, that matter gets into shape

[1] Cazelles' Evolution, p. 32.

when it gets still. But what quiets matter and what makes it integrate or come into shape when it is quiet?"

"It is a law of Nature," replied the skeptic.

"Mill says," rejoined the preacher, "that to explain one law of nature by another, is simply to substitute one mystery for another. We can no more assign a *reason* for the more general laws than for the more partial.[1] And yet, if your reasoning proves anything for science, it proves more for religion."

"How so?"

"Let me show you. Your Nature, with her 'immanent, necessary instinct,' does not perpetuate, as real gains, such transformations as heat into electricity, or of electricity into heat; of gases into rocks, or of rocks into gases; of minerals into vegetables, or of vegetables into animals. In these ebbs and flows of matter, these working correlations change everything and gain nothing."

"I beg your pardon," interrupted the skep-

[1] Mill's Logic, p. 276.

tic, "Nature ever progresses and ever gains. She advanced from chaos and gained organization; she advanced from organization and gained vegetable life; she advanced from vegetable life to animal life."

"Are these gains?" inquired the preacher.

"If they are not, what are?" answered the skeptic. "If you mount by terraces, is not each terrace a gain in altitude, quality of atmosphere, and extent of view? Has not the man on the top of the mountain gained much over the man at its base?"

"Yes, the man at the top, but not the brute in any grade, for whom sublimity is in vain. It needs no lofty tower or mountain-peak to enable it to study the stars in their courses. For it in vain the soft influence of the Pleiads, or the face of Orion or Arcturus. It aspires not from nature to supernature. All it wants is food. For it there need be no loom or spindles. It has appetites, but no desires. Its organization is low, and its future is limited. It never acts upon any ideas, except those which conduce to its two aims, its personal well-being and its propagation; consequently, we may conclude that its brain only resolves a certain class of forces, and that another class appreciated by man are not cognizable by the brute.[1] Like the collodionized plate, the unconscious self registers only one class of phenomena. The beast lives for itself, for its animal nature; it has no other pleasures, for it has no other nature. A horse is indifferent to the rainbow, because the rainbow in no way affects its well-being.[2] The human mind is open to a chain of pleasurable impressions, in no way conducive to the preservation of man's sensual being, and to the perpetuation of his race. He derives pleasure from harmonies of color, and grace of form, and from melodious succession of notes. His animal life needs neither. He is conscious of desires which the gratification of passion does not satisfy, for they

---

[1] Baring Gould's "Origin and Development of Religious Ideas," 51.
[2] Ibid, 5.

are beside and beyond the animal instincts. Man derives his liveliest gratification and acutest pain from objects to which his animal consciousnes is indifferent. The rainbow charms him. Why? Because the sight conduces to the welfare of his spiritual being.[1] The religious instinct, (which is a desire to follow out a law of our being) is the feeling of man after an individual aim other than that of his animal nature.[2] Brute intelligence is not a conscious intelligence, and therefore no gain."

"Does the artist," continued the preacher, "who moulds in clay, consider himself to have gained anything by the image which he breaks? or the painter who thinks in chalk, anything in forms which he rubs out as soon as finished? Can nature be said to have gained anything in individualities which she ever most remorselessly extinguishes? She makes the individual crystal, and dissolves it into gas. She shoots up countless blades of grass, and lifts up the

---

[1] Baring Gould's "Origin and Development of Religious Ideas," 5.
[2] Ibid, 61.

forms of shrub and tree, and draws them back dead into her mysterious workshop. She quickens the pulse of insects, brutes and birds with individual life, and beats them down again in indistinguishable dust, leaving in the universe neither memory nor trace of their individual, unpersonalized existence."

"How do you account for this destructiveness of nature, then?" asked the skeptic.

"Nature, as you scientists present her, uses mere grade and individuality in her manifestations only as a working convenience. Below conscious individuality, which we call personality, no individuality persists. In other words, nature does not regard nor prize mere unconscious individuality as a real advance or gain. If she did, she would not so invariably demolish her work. We do not destroy that which we value. If nature progresses, she does not hold mere individuality to be progress, or she would preserve it. We cannot progress by going back along our own steps."

"Do you consider a man on the mountain top to have gained nothing?"

"Altitude, however high, whose material base may at any moment dissolve beneath the feet and destroy him, is no gain. If man can be lifted from off the mountain top, so that he can abide aloft, upheld by 'Everlasting Arms,' whatever may crumble beneath him, then, and not till then, can he be said to have gained in the movements of existence."

"When nature made individual animals, automatic and intelligent, what else could she make as a gain?"

"She gained consciousness. Why should the 'necessary, immanent instinct,' of which Buckner and yourself speak, having progressed so far, and, as you seem to think, have gained so much, not progress further and gain more? Why should it stop at an unconscious animal? We see that it did not. We see that it went on to the conscious man. Or, why, having lifted the animal upward along the terraces of phenomena, and placed his feet in the frozen dust on the mountain top, not lift his feet still higher, and endow him with power to move like the stars, in individual and perpetual glory, above matter?"

"His feet would then, indeed," said the skeptic, "be ballooning on 'airy nothing.' Better keep them on the solid support of the top terrace."

"I see," replied the preacher, "that you would keep the animal, whether man or brute, on the top terrace, close down to matter."

"What else can he stand on?"

"What," inquired the preacher, "does the top terrace stand on?"

"Why, on the terrace below," replied the skeptic."

"What does the bottom terrace stand on?"

"On— on— FORCE, I suppose."

"Then, if the series of terraces can stand on force below them, why may not man stand on force above them?"

"Force is matter," remarked the skeptic.

"So force is mind," replied the preacher, "yet mind and matter and one kind of force are not identical."

"Prove that," said the skeptic.

"An atom is matter, is it not?"

"Yes."

"The force of gravitation in an atom pulls from the centre of the atom, does it not?"

"Yes."

"In imagination peel off the outside of that atom until you have got down to the centre. You have got down to force, have you not?"

"Yes."

"But where is your matter? You have your force which must transcend matter, but your atom, which was matter, is gone. No, no, my friend. Give up such nonsense as confounding matter and force. They may be associated, but cannot be identical. The man in the saddle is not the same thing as the horse beneath him, which he guides with a bit and bridle. Force guides matter, but is not matter, unless a thing can be said to guide itself, when it is not itself, but something else. Let us come back to common sense. What is there so attractive in matter, or what in it so necessary to personality, that man must be chained to it forever? Blind nature, or your 'immanent necessary instinct,' knows no reason for beginning at matter more than at mind, or for stopping at matter or at mere mind. Why should it not rise and progress forever, and gain forever? If nature began at matter, why should it not go on to mind as we see it did; and if it began in mind, why should it sink back into mere matter? The force that has brought it on from the past is neither exhausted nor bewildered, and can carry it on in the future."[1]

"Do you venture to say," asked the skeptic, "that nature has made anything higher than animal life? If so, what?"

"She made you."

"What is your meaning?"

"To compliment you. Nature, as you call it, rose above the animal, and made you, and me, and all our fellow men."

---

[1] This rather proves that all matter is only manifestations of mind, as so many ancient and modern philosophers have contended. For if matter is force and force is mind, then matter is mind, and so it is no longer matter. Individual phenomena are then only special and changing thoughts.

"How do you prove that men are anything more than a race of animals?"

"By your own admitted principles. You contend that nature ever progresses and gains. Now, the mere animal must, according to this theory, be improved upon, and so on to the summit of being. If blind nature found its way from nothing to a conscious, reasoning man, we can be quite sure that it knows its way to an omniscient God. If a Personal Being did not create nature, nature has, in man, created a personal being. There is a God at one end or the other of progress. The more unconscious things are at the beginning, the more conscious they must be in the end. Development cannot be stopped. If out of nihilism nature evolves life, why should it not out of life evolve immortality? When nature begins, what is to stop her? If she creates many things both in kind and number, she is seen, in all that we observe, to preserve the best. As between individuals and types and forces, is it not according to her most evident way of working that mind-force, as the utilizer of all manifestations of force, should survive as the fittest of all? Whatever else may cease, we cannot suppose that consciousness as the supreme fact in the universe can cease. Nature never inverts the pyramid. Why should conscious, personal mind-force perish, and unconscious, impersonal matter-force survive? In what is the immortal power of the one, and in what is the mortal weakness of the other? Is impersonality superior to personality, or unconsciousness to consciousness? Does the universal thinking of mankind put a *thing* above or on the same level with a *person?* Is a stone superior or equal in the order of nature to Shakspeare, or a vial of electricity to David and Isaiah? Is blindness the honor of nature? Is a mole nearer the summit of her glory than an eagle? Is the idiot more the perfection of nature than Socrates? Such a preference on the part of nature, if it were possible, were the choice of a fool. When the impersonal force defines itself by leaping up into personal or will force, or unconsciousness awakens into consciousness, there would seem to be a gain indeed worth preserving, if anything is. In every sense and for every movement of nature, the personal, the conscious, the coherent, the definite, the moral would be the fittest, both for worth and for struggle. If I were quoting Scripture, I would remind you of the Master's promise, "Because I live, ye shall live also."

"But," continuing the skeptic, "I must insist that the doctrine of the conservation or persistence of force does not prove the immortality of the individual soul. Herbert Spencer says:[1] 'By the persistence of force, we really mean some power which transcends our knowledge and conception. The manifestations, as occurring either in ourselves or outside of us, do not persist; but that which persists is the unknown cause of these manifestations. In other words, asserting the persistence of force is but another mode of asserting an unconditional reality, without beginning or end.'

[1] First Principles, chap. VI, sec 60.

The soul is not a force itself, but only a manifestation of it. The unknown cause persists—the effect perishes."

"This must refer," replied the preacher, "to the manifestation of blind, unintelligent, impersonal force, such as heat, electricity, and gravitation; but as a force, mind and its work, or manifestation, are one and the same. The mind is conscious that it is a power, force, or cause, unto itself; and, of course, takes no knowledge of itself as a mere manifestation, from any cause whatever, known or unknown."

"In reasoning," said the skeptic, "upon the immortality of the soul, from the law of the persistence of type, the persistence of consciousness, and the persistence of force, you pursue three independent, if not conflicting lines of argument."

"I will give up either," remarked the preacher, "if you will admit the sufficiency of the others. These arguments are either all true or all false, or one is true and the others false. That all three are true, you deny. If one be true, it matters not if the others be false. If all are false, as you assume, your dilemma is greater than mine."

"How do you show that?"

"Because, as we know the soul to exist now as a supreme fact, if I fail by either or all of these, your best scientific arguments, to prove the immortality which I affirm, then you must prove the mortality which you affirm. To prove that anything exists, raises the presumption of its perpetual continuance, under any and every possible change. If you deny the presumption, you must prove your denial."

"Your failure is my success. The failure to prove the immortality of the soul establishes its mortality."

"Not at all. The existence of the soul in life is admitted to be the most exalted force in the universe. If you admit that the unconscious, impersonal force, such as electricity or heat, persists, though its presence may be concealed, *a fortiori* you must admit that the greater, more intelligent force of the conscious, personal soul must persist, though its presence may be concealed. Disappearance, in neither case, is destruction. The affirmation that it ceases to exist after death must be proved as an independent proposition by the one who makes it."

"We have no knowledge of it after death," said the skeptic.

"That," replied the preacher, "is no proof that it has ceased to be. Change is not annihilation. Force does not cease because it changes its manifestations, or conceals its presence. When heat is changed into electricity, no force is destroyed. The traveler is not dead because he is out of sight. Existence does not depend on manifestation. Light reveals this world, but it conceals all others. What death is, no one can tell another. It is a secret for each. But science proclaims that everywhere within its searching vision life is triumphant. Reason eagerly explores the field of our own future probabilities, and revelation certifies and glorifies the fact of human immortality. Life is omnipresent. No part of this universe is dead. Life is triumphant. It must be the master, or all things would end. Life is continuous. The one living grain of wheat expands itself into a hundred lives. Death is the last enemy, and life the last friend, in the eternal economy."

"But," replied the skeptic, "admitting a brute to be a mere impersonal individual, and man to be distinguished by having his individuality lifted into what is understood as personal consciousness, and admitting that the soul of man, as mind-force, cannot be annihilated, I still contend that death obliterates its individuality and personality, and reduces both the mind of the individual brute and the mind of the personal man to the same impersonal level of the one universal force. They are but manifestations of force, and are reabsorbed into the eternal abyss of all force. This doctrine of emanation and reabsorption was taught by Aristotle three hundred and fifty years before, and reproduced by Averroes, an Arabian Philosopher of Spain, one thousand two hundred years after Christ, and has been held by the Hindoos in all ages. Is it not Herbert Spencer's theory, too? To me it is the only solution of the life of the soul. With Aristotle, Constructive Reason,[1] as distinguished from Passive Reason,[2] which receives the impression of external things, and perishes with the body, transcends the body, and is capable of separation from it. This Constructive Reason is one individual substance, or universal soul, being one in Socrates, Plato, and other individuals.[3] Whence it follows that individuality consists only in bodily sensations, which are perishable; so that nothing which is individual can be immortal, and nothing which is immortal can be individual."

[1] Herbert Spencer calls this 'Absolute Being,' 'Unknown Cause,' 'Power,' 'Force,' 'Unconditioned Reality, without Beginning or End.' The Athenians call it 'The Unknown God.'
[2] Herbert Spencer calls this 'Manifestations of force which perish.'
[3] What is this but the idea of One God, who breathed in the body of man the breath of life, and he became a living soul, as taught in the Scriptures? Gen. ii: 7.

"I admit," said the preacher, "that while this will answer as well as any other speculation to account for the perishableness of *impersonal* individuality, it is not satisfactory as to the future of *personal* individuality. Vast is the difference upward from an individual *thing* to an individual *person*. Any way, the theory of Aristotle, as reproduced by Averroes, proves too much. It admits that this Constructive Reason is one individual substance. But how, according to this theory, can it be immortal, if it be individual? If individuality destroys immortality, and immortality destroys individuality, then the constructive reason of Aristotle, and even the lauded Nirvana, of the Buddhist, cannot be, because it is both one and immortal."

"I had not thought of that," interrupted the skeptic. "I thought that Aristotle and Averroes, his commentator, proved conclusively that nothing that is individual could be immortal."

"The error of both Aristotle and Averroes, was in antagonizing immortality and personal individuality. It may be conceded that their theory was plausible as to impersonal individuality; but the soul is immortal, according to science, not because it is an individual, but because it is a force, and so, supreme over matter. Above all other force, it has both individuality and personality, and apart from these grand distinctions we know nothing of it."

"But let us go a little further, and see where this extinction of all individuality and personality would land us. Suppose a soul steeped in all possible wickedness to die in the midst of all its vileness, and with the loss of its individuality and personal identity, it is reabsorbed in the great abyss of mind. The Buddhists call this abyss Nirvana. Now the soul must be reabsorbed as it is, bad; not as it is not, good. Ink, if you keep on dropping it long enough, will finally blacken the ocean, and kill all life contained in its illimitable depths. Suppose this absorption to go on for countless ages, bad spirits after bad spirits taken into its very essence; what must Nirvana itself become after feeding so long upon such food, in spite of the good spirits, if any, that may go there too? Its eternal accretions of evil make Nirvana a hell."

"You forget," interrupted the skeptic, "that when the soul loses its individuality, it loses its consciousness, and so escapes suffering."

"On the contrary, in the loss of its individuality and absorption into infinitude consists its horror. For, instead of a finite consciousness which it has lost, it acquires an infinite consciousness which is ever reabsorbing evil. Every soul that it engorges brings in its evil, and makes Nirvana the cess-pool of the universe. This becomes 'hell with a vengeance.'

"Dost thou like the picture?"

"Lo! the hell of reason! I must leave the skeptic, minus his individuality, but plus his Nirvana. And such a Nirvana!"

The skeptic was silent. The preacher continued. "The immortality of the soul, as a preliminary question, having been thus established, though after many and practical diversions, let us now proceed with an examination of the scientific reasons for a belief in a future state of endless punishment, or

2. Hell as a Necessity of Evolution.

(a.) The Law of Grouping Proves a Hell.

"Do you not see, in all nature, a certain behavior of like to like, *similis simili gaudet?* This, in evolution, is known as one of the secondary laws of evolution, called *segregation*. Under this particular movement of evolution, it is shown that in mixed aggregates not only do units of like kind tend to gather together, but units of unlike kind tend to separate. Action and reaction are equal and opposite. Units are repelled from each other by antipathies. The good and the evil mutually repel each other, and the good attracts the good, and the evil attracts the evil. The homogeneous becomes the heterogeneous. The law of like becomes more definite.

"Do not all things assert themselves? Antipathy of evil to good is hell. 'Birds of a feather flock together.' What is the law of chemical affinity but the law of congenial wedlock? Things harmonize together because they suit each other; and things fly off from each other because they do not suit each other. Now, this law of attraction and repulsion runs through all the universe. Heat divorces the worlds, and in its absence, gravitation draws them toward each other. Oil and water will not mix. So with people. They go together very much by congeniality. Moral qualities group them by a fixed law. The vicious naturally run with each other, and the good just as naturally fraternize. Your laws of nature are inexorable and invariable. Account for it as you may, it is so. This is your great Nature God. Just follow this law of like to like out to its eternal consequences, and I think you will have hell enough. It is conjectured that a soul enters the invisible world every second. If one in every ten, or a thousand, or a million, be bad, with low, vile, malicious, beastly appetites and passions, after a while you will have, somewhere in that world, quite a multitude of devils, or one vast master devil, if they return to and poison their source. They would, acting upon your law of nature of like to like, naturally make a local hell.

(*b.*) *The Law of Sympathy or Association.*

"Evil is attracted to evil. Every city has its preliminary hells—its slums, its bar-rooms, where human carcasses lie in beastly stupor, without moral minds, and in rags. The definite becomes more definite. One drunkard knows and consorts with another drunkard. A common shame and love of licentiousness socializes and localizes vile women. Thieves band together with thieves. Human nature must have sympathy and companionship, though that companionship makes a hell apart in its own solitary locality. If one evil spirit bears a mental hell within, two evil spirits make a local hell without. They hunt each other up, and if you think such a set of fiends do not make a local hell, I am sure they do not make heaven anywhere.

"But, then," said the skeptic, "they are to be spiritually changed."

"Now you are getting from your rigid ground of nature to my ground of supernature," said the preacher. "Keep on your plane of science and invariable laws, and leave my side of grace and spiritual help to me."

"Do not be uneasy," replied the skeptic. "I stand by invariable laws."

"Very well, then," continued the preacher, " beside your laws of affinity and associations, or of like to like, there is,

(c.) *The Law of Growth.*

"This is also an awful law in the solution of the destiny of the soul. Look at it in matter. From one little acorn what a sturdy oak will arise, striking its roots deep and wide in the earth, and spreading abroad strong limbs and countless leaves! What a hard, tough, defiant life comes out of that acorn! From one little mustard seed grows a home for the birds. Where two lines meet, how small the angle; but project them into infinity, and how infinitely expanded becomes the included figure. Human imagination cannot depict what one thing, as a cause, may become in its effects. An act is never done acting. Like the pressure of the arch, it never sleeps. Because an act, good or evil, is simply one, it may, though one, like space, embrace a universe.

"All revolutions, riots and reforms are growths from some one idea. Panics, superstitions, popular prejudices, and national animosities are growths. Heretical opinion will mislead long eras under the influence of the law of growth. Evil grows spontaneously. Good must be constantly cultivated. Evil has its natural life in and by us. Good is wrought supernaturally for us. Like the robe of royalty, or the canopy of the skies, it is above and around us—not naturally of us. Besides, kindred to this, look at (d.) *The Law of Propagation.*

"Terrence says : *Fallacia alia aliam trudit:* One falsehood begets another.

"From one acorn comes a whole granary of acorns, each having a new life in its heart. How many grains of wheat may come from one, at each successive planting! Put one cent at interest when a child is born, and what will be the earnings, when the child reaches manhood? A strong bad boy will corrupt a whole school of boys. Now apply these two laws of growth and propagation to the history of a human soul! Their devastation is more readily observed in the career of the drunkard, than in any other. One debauch affects the stomach and destroys the appetite ; it congests the brain and stupefies the mind ; it enervates the will and enfeebles the muscles. The second debauch is still easier, and the third still more easy. This is illustrated in mournful multitudes around us every day. The law of derivation, as applied to evil and its consequences, is inexepressibly horrible.

(e.) The Law of Involution Proves It.

"Every seed inherits a life. This life has two energies — the energy to absorb from the without to the within, and the energy to expand from the within to the without. The first is that of involution or assimilation. This life must appropriate something from the sun, the clouds, and the earth, before its second energy of evolution or expansion from the within to the without, can become active. What it gives out depends on what it takes in. In the language of evolution, this is environment; formerly called the force of circumstances. The life of the seed, having involved or fed upon earth, moisture, and heat, evolves the tree, and transmits the life to other seeds; so, when from inward character, we attract evil associations and absorb from them sin, we develop or evolve that which we have assimilated. Let me quote aptly : 'With the merciful thou wilt show thyself merciful; with an upright man thou wilt show thyself upright; with the pure thou wilt show thyself pure; and with the froward thou wilt show thyself froward.' (18 Ps. xxv : 6.) 'God is not mocked, for whatsoever a man soweth that shall he also reap. For he that soweth to the flesh, shall of the flesh reap corruption; but he that soweth to the spirit, shall of the spirit reap life everlasting.' (Gal. vi : 7.) We may absorb evil or we may absorb good, and the development or evolution will be according to the one or the other. Involution is to take or extract energy *from* our circumstances. Evolution is to give or impart energy *to* our circumstances. The man who takes in good will give out good, and the man who takes in evil will give out evil. The man who associates with a devil will himself become devilish, and one who dwells with an angel will himself become angelic. The maxim is true by the laws of science—a thing is known by its assimilations — 'a man is known by the company he keeps.' These external influences, or environments, change the life in the soul of man, as environments develop and change the life in the seed of the tree. We must involve or take into our life the mind or life of a Christ, if we would evolve his character or move in his lines of happiness.

(*f.*) *The Theory of Evolution.*

" The theory of evolution, or matter without a God, formerly called development, proclaims a way of nature to be in this law of growth, as we have said, that *everything progresses forever.*"

"That is exactly it," interrupted the skeptic; " everything progresses forever. Look along that line and you will see heaven, so far as anything can be seen in the future."

"And you look along that line," said the preacher, " and you will see hell. Evil progresses, results in hell, and the necessity to progress forever makes that hell eternal."

"The sins of the body cannot progress forever, for they cease with the death of the body," remarked the skeptic.

"Yes," replied the preacher, " but the sins of the mind will progress forever, for they continue with the life of the mind."

"As from the bottom of the hill the grade is upward, so from the top of the hill the grade is downward. In the law of change—detected by the ceaseless search of science—there is an eternal devolution or movement downward, as well as an eternal evolution or movement upward. The science of humanity shows three things: First—That human nature is down close to animals and fiends, and tends still lower. Second—That it needs to be helped up, for it cannot rise of itself. And third—That when up, it needs to be held up, for it cannot hold itself up. This is evident in the decline of men, schools of thought, and conquering races. There is no Solon in the Areopagus, or Socrates in the streets of Athens, nor Cicero in the Forum, or Cæsar at the Capitol of Rome. The scepter has departed from Judah. The falling off of genius, as shown in the science or history of heredity, shows that there is no self-elevating power inherent in human nature. An eminent man is a surprise to the race. He is wondered at as a prodigy, if not adored as a god. He has no successor. His descendants may be fools or fiends. If his great ability descends, it will be with a flickering light, and, as a rule, in the fourth generation go entirely out. Let the degradation go on, and the race wind up in human devils, for whom we men have prisons on earth and science a hell hereafter. That the law of human nature is to fall, not rise, is evident from the history of pauper individuals, the rapid deterioration of aristocratic families, however gifted by nature and favored by circumstances. All flattery of human nature and applause of distinguished exceptions, is directly in the teeth of the honest conclusions of science. Humanity is a failure, and science, with no practical remedy to offer, is amazed in the presence of the fact. Rejecting the merciful help of the Redeemer, science seeks to struggle alone with the mournful doom which is even now upon man; and for the glorious, comforting, and regenerating hope of the one, we are left in the cold, dark despair of the other. Science lights the way to an inevitable hell, and scornfully rejects all revealed helps to a Savior's heaven."

"Still," observed the skeptic, "God (your God) is a Father."

"Still," echoed the preacher, "these are facts. Your idea of the Fatherhood of God is all wrong ; nor is your idea of the sovereignty of God all right. When not so ignorant of yourself, you will know more of God. Obedient children have loving fathers, but rebellious citizens have stern rulers. God is a Father, and God is a Sovereign, and yet human nature runs down ; and so persistent is the law of devolution that it runs down in spite of secular and repressive force, and under the very shadow of the Cross itself."

"Why does not God stop it?" sneeringly inquired the skeptic.

"Why does not the new religion of science stop it?" replied the preacher. "Science has full opportunity to arrest the declension of human nature, but no power ; God has the power to regenerate human nature and lift it up, but in the blindness of science and the perverseness of the human heart, He has slight opportunity. He does all that man will let him do."

"Suppose," said the skeptic, "that a man reforms his evil life?"

"What will make him do it?" inquired the preacher.

"Improvement in knowledge."

"Has it ever done it?"

"Experience of the disadvantage of evil, then, will," said the skeptic.

"Has that ever done it? According to your invariable, inexorable laws of nature, (with no God behind them) things have no power to stop themselves. They evolve because they must. Your law is that everything, including evil, progresses forever. Do not back out from your law. Stand by it. You have nothing left but—"

"Hell, you would say?" interrupted the skeptic.

"There is nothing else from your standpoint," replied the preacher. "Everything progresses forever. If you project a ball, it will go on forever unless something else stops it; it cannot stop itself, nor can it change itself. For matter to change, it must be combined with some other matter. Oxygen, by itself, will ever remain oxygen, and hydrogen, by itself, will ever remain hydrogen; but combine the two and they become water. But in themselves they are inert."

"How is it as to mind?" asked the other.

"It, too, goes on, and forever. As a force, it cannot go out. It may change its sphere, but not its essence or its office. All that we see and know of mind is as a force and an individuality. Each one is conscious that his mind is his own, and not another's. The creed of evolution is intensification, integration, persistence. We know as much of the individuality of the mind as we know of the mind itself. The consciousness of the mind and its individuality is one and the same. We may as well expect the mind itself to perish, as to expect its individuality and personality to perish. The mind can make itself, generically, no other thing than it is. It is mind, and not matter; and mind, and not matter, it must ever be. Whatever it is, it is so as an individual. As nature never abdicates itself, mind can never surrender or extinguish itself, or be less mind; but your laws of nature compel it to be more mind, whether good or bad. It must progress fearfully in evil or gloriously in good."

"I suppose," said the skeptic, "that is the way you get into your heaven."

"Never mind that; but this is the way," replied the preacher, " that you get into your hell. The evil in man grows into the infinite in evil, and that is a hell; and many evil spirits associating together, upon the law of like to like, make a local hell; more of a hell than any brimstone could make it. To return, then, to their source, only poisons it yet the more, and the Persian Ahriman, or God-devil, results.

"But I deny," said the other, "that anything survives that is not worth surviving."

"The truth of science teaches something

more," responds the preacher. "The science of the present teaches us to expect in the future the survival of the worst as well as the best. Each survives by a life of its own, and the survival of one does not require the death of the other—at least, it is so in this world, and why not in the next? Wicked men prosper as well as the good. Weeds destroy flowers. Wise laws do not make all citizens virtuous. The knowledge of the rule does not inspire us with a love for the principle. Civilization changes the crime, but not the criminal. Education lifts the thieving boy into the forging man. We have the Declaration of Independence, and the threat of the Commune. Evil changes its name, but not its nature."

"But," says the skeptic, "evil forfeits individuality."

"Evil, in the sense of sin, belongs to character, and forfeits only happiness. Personal individuality, whether the creation of evil or an evolution of law, pertains to existence, and endures forever. According to material science, nature is no moralist, and knows nothing of good or evil. As all phenomena with her are invisible successions rather than voluntary departures, so there can be no forfeitures, because there is no disobedience. With her there are sequences, but no consequences; and everything is material and nothing moral. And so the soul cannot be annihilated because it is evil, nor exist forever because it is good."

"A soul," continued the preacher, " is not annihilated because it is evil. As it is not immortal because it is individual, so it is not immortal because it is good. It exists not because it is either good or an individual, but because, according to science, it is a force, and cannot perish. The mind is no less a force because it is evil ; but for that reason it is a more terrible force. It is a force because it is mind, irrespective of all moral considerations, and as such force it is imperishable. Evil has a law of growth as well as good. If this reasoning be correct, we have in the human soul, saturated with evil, an imperishable, ever-growing intelligence, incapable of suicide. As neither matter nor mind, according to modern science, can stop itself, it is under the inevitable necessity, unless some supreme force intervene, as the hand arrests the descending ball, to fall forever and forever, beyond the unfathomable depth of the infinite line of even transcendental geometry.

"No atom inherits power. Power is a gift to everything. Like a world once out of its orbit that must go on increasing the troubles incident to its misbehavior, so the soul must, according to science, keep on in evil or good until it is stopped. Every atom has its own place. Suppose it to step disobediently out of its place for one brief second, what would be the result? All rays of light would be mixed and darkened; all waves of sound would be obliterated and silenced; the circuits of the winds would become confused; the unpoised planets would hurtle in the void immense; the earth insanely plunge amidst the unutterable horrors; all leaves would wither and die; all beauties become hideous to behold; all life expire, and the whole universe become one hell of quivering matter, and so continue until readjusted by the original force of the first intelligence. This is the truth of science.

" When the mind steps out of its place and function, there is madness. The soul, in its proper sphere, has ultimate happiness; out of its proper sphere, is ultimate hell.

" The soul of man—by which is here meant all in him not material—is a force, like all force, solemnly everlasting. As to impersonal, unconscious, willess force, unknown apart from matter, it cannot disobey; and if it did, it could not suffer. But it is far otherwise with soul-force. It is free to determine within and for itself whether it will agree or disagree with other forces, whether in nature or supernature. If the former, it is in harmony; if the latter, it is in discord, and all discord is so much hell.

" As everything, unresisted, progresses forever, so the soul-force must, by its nature, develop to infinity the good or evil it chooses.

And it differs from all blind force in that it has its *power of choice*. As the presence of matter-force is always equal to the quality and relations of matter, so soul-force develops in a good or bad direction according to the opportunity and the absence of restraint. The soul, which is ever somewhere, makes its own local hell. The question is not whether some unmerciful Superior plunges man into everlasting punishment; but the question is, how far will some merciful Superior prevent man, in his immortality as a soul-force and his willful progress in evil, from plunging himself? All nature inquires of man, with the emphasis of woe, 'Why will you be eternally miserable?' Now, observe the relentless hell of science, without mercy, hope or end! It indignantly denies, by its axioms, that the soul can be annihilated. Nature drops nothing. Evil has no power in itself to change itself, and science worships no God who would change it. Evil must continue evil, and suffering must ever be suffering. Science makes Nature a dreadful, merciless monarch, indeed! Nature never retraces its steps. Nothing that we say, or do, or think, or are, can be obliterated. It must ever remain and develop. 'Everything progresses forever,' shouts the Angel of Evolution to Virtue, to encourage its flagging energies. And 'everything progresses forever,' warns remorseless Evolution to vice as it chafes under supernatural restraint. As an atom out of its material place convulses all the material forces, so does a soul out of its moral place disturb all moral forces. The one creates disturbance, and is a hell in matter. The other creates mental horrors, and it is a hell in mind. God creates no hell for man, but warns him from his own. Man is his own hell, not from remorse, but for his evil for which he has no remorse. Remorse arrests not sin. Remorse is the least of hell. Hell is in the evil which causes remorse. As the oak is but an unfolded acorn, so hell is but expanded or unfolded sin. As the sea is but the cistern of the rivers, so hell is but the cistern of sin. To be warned of hell is not sufficient. Every evil is a blind giant, ignorant of itself, heedless of warnings, and almost defiant of resistance, and unapproachable by help. A man is warned that drunkenness will becloud the mind, bestialize the body, and ruin fortune and fame. He does not heed the warning. He drinks yet deeper. To suffer does not reform. He actually suffers indescribable agonies, yet he will not heed. Others, most dear to him, wife and children, suffer on his account, yet he drinks. It is even worse with lust. The impure touch makes the leper. How often do we see parents going down to their graves in sorrow because of the dreadful power of some ruinous sin upon a precious child, that would not, and finally, perhaps, cannot, cease to do evil? Indeed, science is mournfully true: 'unresisted, everything progresses forever.' The evil mind is an architect that hourly adds another and another block to the wall of the eternal prison in which it chains itself. Evil continued until its consequences are felt—this is so much hell.

"But we have no time to exhaust the argument. No figure ever equals the fact, as we have said, so no description of the outcome of evil in the universe equals the reality. Human language is inadequate to the task. The laws proclaimed by science prove that man, through evil in his nature, makes a hell for himself in that locality where his evil peculiarities ultimately consign him, to that of which fire and brimstone is no exaggerated comparison."

"You put it strong," said the skeptic.

"Suffering makes all places hell—just as mental suffering is greater than bodily suffering, so its hell is worse," said the preacher. "We have been taught that hell is a locality; and so it is. The shadow and the beam have each its place. But, as a village is nothing to an empire, to a continent, to a hemisphere; as the centre is nothing to the circumference; as a point is nothing to all space; so is the placed hell of past teachings as nothing to the unplaced hell of science. To the evil 'all places are hell.' Hell is in the presence of broken law, whether in mind or matter, in time or eternity. It is where heaven is not. There is nothing more ubiquitous or relentless than Nature's pursuit and punishment of disobedience. Nature brands all offenders, and never lets up; never forgets or forgives; never stops striking direct or consequential blows. 'The mind is its own place.' To the maniac, moral or mental, there is omnipresent horror; fire and water, light and darkness, are alike the 'lake of brimstone' and the 'undying worm.' And to science there is no escape, no mercy, no pardon, no sympathy, no change, no death. Science shows that all things, even evil, are horribly persistent.

"The pain (*punishment*) of it may be 'everlasting.' But, since Christ came, yea, since He was promised, man need not endure it for one second hereafter. Evolution is a continuous effect from a continuous cause, or the persistence of operative law; but even effects, as distinguished from the process of evolution, if you choose to make such a distinction, survive the causes that originate them. A moment of sin oftentimes plants disease that no time can efface. The pain will be as long as the life. So, in the other world, the pain is as long as the sin. Pain (punishment) expires when the sin expires; but when is that to be, apart from the blood of Christ, which alone cleanses from all sin? Sin is never exhausted from any inherent weakness. The disgrace of a crime which it took but a moment to commit, is indelible upon reputation and happiness. Christ intervened to save the guilty, even with his life. When this proves unavailing, evil proves in them an everlasting persistence, whether you consider it an evolution or an effect; and when that failure is finally ascertained, the soul is no longer that of a child, but that of an enemy. Then it will go where enemies go. As a vile thing, it will go with the vile. Of one thing we may be certain, and that is, that God will keep every soul out of pain as long as that exemption will avail. But if he exhausts his means *here*, he need not repeat them *there*. God does not hurl the wicked into punishment; they 'go away' into fires made everlasting—not for man, but for the devil. Thus—

The Law of Affinity proves a hell.
The Law of Association proves it.
The Law of Growth proves it.
The Law of Propagation proves it.
The Law of Involution proves it.
The Law of Evolution proves it.

"As has been said, great mercy implies great guilt, and great guilt can hardly complain of great injustice, whatever may be the sentence.

"'In the eternal fitness of things' God saves his children from everything they ask him to save them from—yes, from every pain they will permit him to save them from. Even if through inexperience and unbelief men commit the sins they wish to commit, they take the risk of the pain, not realizing that every sin *involves* a violation of a law of happiness, and *evolves* a consequent pain. Christ bore our pain (Isa. lviii.) If we refuse Him, what have we left? Though a creature of limited freedom, man's future is necessarily and ultimately very much in his own hands.

> Life is an endless curse—
> Life is an endless bliss—
> Life in the other world
> Is as we choose in this.

"Having considered hell as a place anywhere and everywhere out of heaven, and as an effect from disobedience as a cause, let us now consider pain: first, as a *means* that God, the Father, uses to bless us; second, as a *result* from our own character."

"Consider what you like," said the skeptic, "I will hear you on."

II.

The Pain (*Punishment*) which our Heavenly Father Visits upon his Children of Earth is Always as a Means, and Never as an End.

"But," says the skeptic, "suppose I do believe in my individual immortality? Suppose I believe in a personal God—a Father to all his creatures, and of too benevolent a nature to doom one of them to everlasting torments for the sins of this short life?"

"Ah!" says the preacher, "we are now to consider the moral economy of an infinite Person, rather than the blind evolution of merely infinite Power. Some moral factors now come into view. You believe there is a distinction between right and wrong?"

"Yes," answers the skeptic.

"Suppose a soul does wrong, how does the wrong act affect his life?"

"He suffers for it here."

"Does suffering reform the soul? Criminals are chronic sufferers, and are not thereby the least improved or purified."

"But," it was replied, "suppose that in the other world, we shall have more light, and think as our Heavenly Father would have us?"

"You then believe with Socrates, that if men knew the right they would certainly do it."

"Yes; I think Socrates one of the greatest men that ever lived."

"Does not the thief," remarked the preacher, "who steals your watch, know that he is doing wrong? If he knows no better, he can do no better; why do you punish him?"

"I admit that intellectual knowledge is not moral power," answered the skeptic; "but I must come back to the proposition, that God—and I admit one for the sake of the argument—is too good to create a vast lake, and kindle up an inextinguishable fire of brimstone, or construct any other similar horror in which to put his child. Would you, as a parent, put your child in any such place, even for one second, much less for eternity, no matter what he might have done? I know you would not. Nor has God any such future for any of his creatures."

"I am glad to hear you so earnest in your appreciation of the Fatherhood of God. He is a Father so long as we are children; but when we become irreverent, ungrateful and vicious, what do you say as to his sovereignty?"

"His sovereignty—nonsense!" says the skeptic.

"You break one of his laws, and see if there be any nonsense in the result," replies the preacher. "God loves, but he rules, and it would be a dark day for the universe if he ceased to rule."

"True," quickly responds the skeptic; "he rules by general, invariable laws, that neither turn nor cease."

"You believe in these laws, do you?" inquired the preacher.

"As firmly as you do."

"Thanks ; we can now go on—"

"To hell?" sarcastically inquires the skeptic?"

"Not with me, I trust," replied the preacher; "if you go there you must go alone. Neither God nor man sends you there. You simply go by the urgency of something evil within you."

"By what law? If God has put within me a law that sends me to your hell, I would curse him and die. As you represent God," continued the skeptic, "you make him an unjust and merciless monster. Is it just to make the one sin of Adam, in which no one feels any participation, and for which no one feels personally responsible, the ground of the death, whether temporary or eternal, of every or of any descendant of Adam? Is this the award of your God of pity?"

"We claim that, although men had sinned and brought death into our world, yet God so loved the world that he gave his only begotten Son, that whosoever believeth in him should have everlasting life. But looking at the matter as you do, has nature, which is to you what my God is to me, any more justice or pity?" replied the preacher. "Death is here, with or without a reason. If nature brings death, and nature has no reason for it, then nature is a monster. If nature has a reason, what is it?"

"It is as natural to die as to be born," said the skeptic. "Death is not a punishment based on moral reasons, but an ordinance of nature, sin or no sin. Why should your God kill a little bird for the sin of Adam?"

"Why," replied the preacher, "should your nature kill a little bird for no sin at all, of any one? We say that man sinned, and death came into the world as a consequence. You say that sin, if there be any, had nothing to do with it. Instead of believing that there is a God who smites with a reason, you prefer to believe that there is no God, and nature smites without a reason. Any way, your bitterness will not help you to light," quietly remarked the preacher.

1. FALSE IDEAS OF THE FATHERHOOD OF GOD.

"In our last talk respecting the fact and locality of hell," said the skeptic, "you spoke of evil having no power within to stop itself, and you illustrated your idea by alluding to a falling ball, which would fall forever, unless arrested by some other body or some resistive force. How, then, according to such views of the nature of things, can any one be saved?"

"That's a problem for you skeptics to answer. I confess that, looking at the constitution of things as you do, I do not see how any one can be saved."

"But," insisted the skeptic, "suppose I am persuaded of the immortality of the soul—of the distinction between right and wrong—of the punishment here for all the wrongs we commit—and of the existence of a God; do you think it possible for him to punish forever, in burning brimstone, one of his poor, weak, blind children of earth, for acting, sinfully if you choose to call it so, in the line of weakness which He himself gave?"

"So changeable are the objections of skepticism," replied the preacher, "that it is no easy task to run them all down. They come around in periods, and rage as epidemics. As the stomach, long fed upon dainties, becomes morbid, so the mind, long cultivated in subtle speculation, leading to no satisfactory conclusions, becomes dyspeptic and despairing. One puts himself down on the plane of nature among the bugs and stones and trees, and tries to persuade himself that he will die, and like

> 'Imperious Cæsar, dead, and turned to clay,
> Might stop a hole to keep the wind away.'

"Another hopes to rise from nature to supernature, and,

> 'aloft ascending, breathe in worlds
> To which the heaven of heavens is but a veil.'"

"You but aptly describe the future of the human soul, if it has a future," earnestly added the skeptic. "I expect for myself and all of my race, upon the theory of the immortality of the soul, an eternity of happiness prepared by a Father of infinite love and wisdom for all his children alike. Our Heavenly Father would no more put one of his children in everlasting fire than you would put the end of your child's finger in the fire for one minute. Would he? Now answer me candidly, as a father, and not as an advocate trying to make out a case. It is a pity for the progress of truth in the world that you preachers have to pretend to believe so much, and argue against what must be your convictions, to keep up your churches and salaries."

"Most preachers can make far more at anything else than they do at preaching; but," continued the preacher, "let us keep to the question. You form your idea of God's fatherhood from the sentiments, shortsightedness and weaknesses of your own fatherhood."

"Well, how else," inquired the skeptic, "can I form an idea of God's fatherhood? Do you not say that I am made in his image?"

"If you are," replied the preacher, "the mould got a flaw in it before the cast was made. It is rather a slur on God to say, because we have started in his image, that we are so now. The world has never seen anything particularly divine in the Benedict Arnolds, and Neros, and Judases, and no one ever supposed that the cells of San Quentin were cloisters of the gods, or any very near kin to them. But let me ask you a few questions: You would not let your child writhe under the toothache, if you could help it, would you?"

"No, of course," answered the skeptic.

"God does let his children have a thousand toothaches," answered the preacher. "You would not let your child groan under the burdens of poverty, would you?"

"You can well suppose I would not," replied the skeptic.

"God not only lets his children be poor," said the preacher, "but he lets them starve, and go naked, and houseless, though he gives the birds their nests in the trees, and the foxes their holes in the ground. You would not let your children get drunk, steal, and rob, and go into prison, if you could help it, would you?"

"To ask such a question," said the skeptic, "is to answer it."

"Finally, you would not let your children sicken and die, and be put in the cold ground and . decay. You would employ the most learned skill to cure them, and undertake the most expensive and distant journeys to keep them in health. And yet God, able to do far more abundantly than we can ask or think, lets all his children suffer all this. Do you not think your ideas of the fatherhood of God are a little mixed?" inquired the preacher.

"Mixed with what?" replied the skeptic.

"Mixed with the ideas of your own fatherhood," answered the preacher.

"Do not the Scriptures and you preachers teach us to look at fatherhood in that way?" inquired the skeptic, with a tone of rebuke.

"Not at all," replied the preacher. "Ideas of fatherhood are according to grade of life.

A pig's idea of fatherhood, so far as he has any, is to teach his offspring to eat, lie down, and root in filth. The bee's idea of fatherhood is to teach its little ones to hunt for honey, and providently put away something for winter. The eagle's idea of fatherhood is to teach its eaglet to turn its eye up to the sun, and to show it how, upon defiant wing, to ride the storm, and lose itself as a palpitating spot above the lightning's home. Man's too common idea of fatherhood is merely to refine his child's tastes, give him graceful indulgences, and enable him to live without work. How few attempt to lift the thoughts of their children to any considerations above or beyond this world!"

"What is God's idea of fatherhood?" interposed the skeptic.

"We know most imperfectly the mind of God," replied the preacher. "Nature tells us nothing of this fatherhood of God. There is no idea of fatherhood in the fetish worship of a stone, or a bug, or a rag; none in the worship

THE FATHERHOOD OF GOD. 149

of holy wells, sacred springs and rivers; none in the druidical worship of the oak; none in the Northman's worship of the wolf and the bear; none in the Egyptian worship of the serpent and the crocodile; none in the Eastern worship of fire and the sun; none in the Chaldean's worship of the stars."

"But," asked the skeptic, "does not David say that God is a father to the fatherless?"

"Yes, and so he is to all who are, or behave like, children; but he is a sovereign to all who behave like criminals."

"Does not Paul speak of him as 'the father of mercies'?"

"Yes. He is rich in mercy to all proper subjects of mercy who *call* upon him. Mercy points the penitent to a happy life, and rejected mercy points the impenitent to a horrible doom; great mercy implies great guilt, and great guilt evolves a great wretchedness. Mercy can only come into play when it is in the power of a superior to punish or pardon. But if there can be no future suffering, and all go to the same place, the soul can laugh at both God's threat of punishment and his offer of pardon. There would then be no need of mercy, because there would be no danger.

"Yet, I confess that I do not know how to take you. You are sometimes on one system and then on another. If I talk of God answering prayer, or of his providence, you reply to me the general, invariable laws of the universe, and reject with skeptical scorn the idea of God suspending a general law to answer a special wish or prayer of his children. And if I speak of the laws of force, and of personal affinity, and association and evolution, and so on, leading to an inevitable hell in the very nature of things, you cry out God is a good Father, and all that. Now, the more God governs by law the more he is sovereign, and the less he is paternal. The more paternal he is, the less does he govern by law. Law is on the sovereign side of his character, and his fatherhood is on the affectionate side. You make him all father or all sovereign, according to the exigency of your argument. The more father the less law, and the more law the less father. Make your choice, and stand by it."

"Does not David speak of the Lord pitying his creatures, even as a father pitieth his children?"

"Not exactly that. Let me quote Scripture my own way, and I can prove anything out of them. You skeptics, and some preachers, hastily put out sentiments as Scripture which are not so at all. David said, 'Like as a father pitieth his own children, even so the Lord is merciful unto them that *fear* him.'

"Now, be frank with me, my skeptical friend, and answer me truly: Do not all who believe in universal salvation, or universal and final restoration, which some so-called orthodox people believe, think that no matter what they do—steal, drink, kill, debauch the pure, ruin families, oppress the poor and the helpless, lie, betray friends and country—that the Lord cannot help himself—that he has but one place to put them. Do they *fear* him at all? Do they ever even talk about *fearing* him? Not at all."

"What, then," asked the skeptic, are the

2. True Ideas of God's Fatherhood as to Pain?"

"'Ye have forgotten the exhortation which speaketh unto you as unto children,'" replied the preacher. "'My son, despise not thou the chastening of the Lord, nor faint when thou art rebuked of him, for whom the Lord loveth he chasteneth, and scourgeth every son whom he receiveth. If ye endure chastening, God dealeth with you as sons; for what son is he whom the Father chasteneth not? But if ye be without chastisement whereof all are partakers, then are ye bastards, and not sons. Furthermore, we have had fathers of our flesh which corrected us, and we have given them reverence. Shall we not much rather be in subjection unto the Father of Spirits, and live? For they, verily, for a few days chastened us after their own pleasure, but he *for our profit*, that we might be partakers of his holiness. Now, no chastening, for the present, seemeth to be joyous, but grievous; nevertheless, afterward it yieldeth the peaceable fruit of righteousness unto them which are exercised thereby.' (Heb. xii: 5-11.) Now our profit is the end for which our Father uses the means of pain.

" (*a.*) *God uses Pain as a Present Teacher.*— Pain prompts thought. The disciple is a learner, and discipline is education. All animals seem to take knowledge mostly in this way. The pain of hunger and disease, and of bodily exposure, makes all creatures, from the lowest to the highest, actively provident. By the fear of pain, we often discipline the brutes that serve us, and by that fear we are safe from those that would otherwise destroy us. Pain leads to knowledge.

"(*b.*) *God uses Pain as a Corrective.*—He chastises us to chasten or purify us. This is designed to make that right in us which was wrong before. If the knowledge of what was
7*

best for our happiness, forced upon us in *discipline*, led to a change of inner principle, *corrective* pain would be unnecessary. But, knowledge is not principle. If the pain which God visits upon us in mercy to enlighten us through discipline and purify us through chastisements fail, then

(*c.*) *God uses Pain to Restrain our Acts.*—This is merciful to ourselves and others. There comes a point in the history of human life when God makes the barrier of pain say to us, 'Thus far, but no further.' If knowledge will not stop us, if no new principles can be implanted in us by corrective pain, then arises the necessity of restraining pain. This is all parental. Like any other father, God uses no more pain than the case requires. If he uses more than we would, it is because he sees more to be necessary than we see, and that no less would answer. The weakness of the human heart makes it ' spare the rod and spoil the child.' There are children so incorrigible that even human love neither disciplines any more, nor corrects any more, but simply restrains when it can. It is as a means to these ends, and for this world, that God causes pain. The pain in the world to come is our own act. God stands in the way, and says, 'Turn ye, turn ye; why will ye die?' 'Whosoever cometh unto me I will in no wise cast out.' How affectionately he pleads with us, even as many an earthly father pleads with a child, to be wise and safe. He seeks to protect his creatures as a hen gathereth her chickens under her wings. He has sent sacred kings, inspired prophets, and his only Son and his blessed Spirit, to turn men from sin and misery. What more could he have done that he has not done? Neither his goodness nor his severity avail."

III.

Pain (*Punishment*) Endless as a Result of Character — Man's Own Act.

1. OF HIS WILL, MAN REFUSES THE GIFT.

"To give salvation is God's part—to take it, man's. 'Ye will not come to me, that ye might have life.' (John v : 40.) 'I have called, but ye have refused.'

"I suppose," said the skeptic, "you think that

2. AT THE JUDGMENT, SOULS ARE SEPARATED ACCORDING TO CHARACTER."

"'He shall separate them,'" said the preacher, "' one from another, as a shepherd divideth the sheep from the goats. And he shall set the sheep on his right hand, and the goats on the left.' Now, these on the left are those incorrigible spirits, to whom the discipline of life in vain gave the knowledge of duty to God, to themselves, and to others—in whom the corrections of the Father wrought no purification —who resisted the good persuasions of the Spirit—who were insensible to the mission of the Son—whom God could not make better people, consistent with their freedom, and was compelled, so to speak, to restrain them, in life and time. Now, what is to be done with them? They would yield to nothing in life but the restraint of pain, and what else will they yield to in eternity? By character they are not fit for heaven; but where else can they go? Notice, that God does not then curse them. When he says 'Depart, ye cursed,' he does not *doom*, but only *describes* them. He makes no new state, but simply announces the old one man made for himself. Their incorrigible character is their curse. As even man saw that nothing would make them better in time, so God sees that nothing will make them better in eternity. God has shown his desire to save them, but he says unto them here and now, 'Ye will not come unto me, that ye might have life.' For the devil and his angels God provided a hell, anticipating its necessity, but offered no salvation, as that would have been useless to such terrible offenders; but for man he provided a salvation, anticipating, as it were, its universal acceptance, and of course provided no place of punishment. As man had followed Satan in time, there was no alternative but to make him his companion for eternity. Like to like. Each one goes to his own place—to the place and condition most suitable to his character. From Christ's known attribute of love, we may suppose that there will be no vengeance in his tone when he, as the Judge, shall say: 'I called, but ye refused;' depart, you who have cursed yourselves, who have made yourselves incurably vile; depart to the only place suitable to you—to a place prepared, not for you, but for the devil and his angels.

'And these shall *go* away into everlasting punishment, (or pain) but the righteous into life eternal.'"

IV.

Salvation God's Act in One of Three Ways.

"Now, as I look at it," continued the preacher, "there is but one of three ways by which man can be saved.

1. As a Destiny.

"(*a.*) *Universal at Death.* — According to some, after man, like the falling ball, began to run down in moral and spiritual life, he was arrested by a decree of destiny. It was ordered, without consulting him, without any merit on his part, that he should stop falling, and begin to rise toward and ultimately into heaven."

"Well," inquired the skeptic, "why is not that a good way? Man has no trouble with that sort of an arrangement. He was falling before, because having gotten into the downward grade he could not help himself, and this way of destiny is only the reverse movement. Some foreign power takes hold of a lost soul, turns it round, and starts it upon the opposite course, along which it must go, whether it will or no. I rather like that way. What is the objection to it?"

"There certainly seems to be this one," replied the preacher: "to turn man before he wants to turn, makes heaven a necessity. A necessary heaven, constituted as man is, becomes a necessary hell. Constraint begets no love. Where love is not, heaven is not. If the immortal spirit finds no hell in the eternal spaces of God, it will not thank God for the gift of a heaven he could not withhold. It would claim heaven to be its own appropriate necessity, as much as God's. Thence would arise the bold assertion of equality with God, because God and man would be equally and inevitably happy, though differing in moral worth as widely as good and evil. As heaven is God's personal home, if there be no hell, then God would be compelled to stay there with all the wicked souls who rebelled against him and defied his power. They never would grow better in heaven, for there would be no motive to repent. God would have to keep them there, for, if there be no hell, there would be nowhere else to put them. This would not make a heaven for the bad, but it would make a hell for the good. I don't think that God is so scant of space that he could not get out of that society. But there is no danger of such a predicament. The wicked can no more obtrude upon the society of God, than darkness can invade the sun. If destiny thrusts salvation on some, and compels them to be saved, I do not see why destiny could not be amiable about it and thrust it on all, and compel all to be saved as well as a few."

"Well, that is exactly what I say," responded the skeptic. "What can hair-splitting reasoning answer to that?"

"Why, simply this," remarked the preacher, "salvation, by compulsion, is no salvation."

"Do you mean to say that if God were to coerce man into salvation, he would be perverse, and defeat God's benevolent intentions?"

"Something like that. Constituted as man is, a benefit you compel man to accept is not valued, and ceases to be a benefit to him. Man values most that which he longs for, and begs for, and fights for."

(*b.*) *The Destiny of Universal Salvation by the Final Restoration of all Souls.*—" As to God's laws," said the skeptic, " do they not work out an ultimate restoration of all things? From decay, does there not come a new life? Does not light succeed the darkness? Are we not to have a new heavens and a new earth?"

"Yes, but that is to create something new, not reconstruct or restore anything old, which is to be burnt up," answered the preacher, " but the theory of evolution remorselessly forbids restoration. The barbed arrow may go forward, but not backward. Evolution may develop a thing that has a start, but not make it something else. To be restored we must be changed. If man can change in the other world, either he must change himself from within, which I say, according to the laws of evolution, is impossible, or be changed from without, which you say, also according to the laws of evolution, is impossible."

"Why do you say that change from within is impossible?" inquired the skeptic.

"Because," answered the preacher, "the change must be so great as to amount to a new creature, and transmutation is unknown in nature. Iron cannot metamorphose itself into gold, nor tares into wheat. There is a difference between restoring old things and creating new ones. God could regenerate what man degenerates; but that would conflict with evolution, and make restoration come from help without, which evolution denies, as all its energies are from within."

"Please give me, in a few words," said the

skeptic, "your ideas of evolution, which seems to be your horror."

"It is not my horror, at all," replied the preacher. "It matters not what evolution is, God is its master. But, to answer your question. Definitions differ as to what evolution is. Anything evolved is, like a blush, evolved from a thought within or behind it. The evil soul can evolve only evil thoughts, just as water cannot rise above its own level. - Evolution, as before said, is an unfolding. It is not the substitution of one thing for another, but simply more of the same thing. Evil cannot be evolved into good, nor good into evil. There may be an obliteration of the one, and a substitution of the other; but that would be a divine act, not a blind evolution. Evolution requires an evil soul to progress forever, and admits of no change which could be called restoration.

"But there is another view of this hope of ultimate restoration which has a frightful outlook, and it is this: the principle that admits the possibility of departed spirits changing themselves, or of being changed in the future world, threatens to depopulate heaven quite as much as it promises to exhaust hell. If the bad man can become good hereafter, (as I could wish) and finally be saved, may not the good possibly become bad hereafter, and finally be lost? As man is more inclined to evil than to good, there is solemn danger that the natural possibility of change after death, instead of restoring the bad, would only endanger the safety of the good. What the Bible says about this whole matter, is another thing."

"Keep to the field of law," said the skeptic.

"Very well," replied the preacher, "I prefer to stick to that line of argument, or confessedly change it to some other, but not attempt to be on both sides of the fence at once. But, as you insist that we shall continue to argue on the side of law, let me ask, Are these laws changeable or unchangeable?"

"Why, unchangeable, of course," was the skeptic's prompt reply.

"Then," replied the preacher, "there can

be no restoration. Blind law cannot change itself. It can design nothing. It cannot prefer one thing to another. It cannot divert things into new departures, because it has no intelligence, and can see no necessity for a new departure. To it, death and decay are the same as life and renewal. According to that nature of things which so attracts and deludes you, a soul, like a fall, enters eternity on the downward grade, with no power within to stop itself. Now if, with all the motives it had in this world, it did not stop, what is to stop it there? Some foreign power must intervene. But if it yielded to no other intervention here, when it had persuasions of the most affecting nature, can it hope for more there? If tares will not turn into wheat while they stand in a field of wheat, is it more likely that they will turn into wheat when they are off in a field by themselves? Is it not more likely that bad people will amend when they are associating with the good, than when they are all grouped off by themselves? It seems to me that when bad spirits draw off in the other world from all the restraints and persuasions that surround them here, their chance for restoration becomes every second less and less. And the probability of their restoration, according to the terrible laws of science, becomes inversely less according to the square of time and distance from the isolations of the evil at death. If the chance of restoration one year after death be, say 2 less, at two years it would be 4, at three years it would be 16, and so on until there would be no chance at all. And we see this law at work here. The more we indulge in sin, the more we can indulge. Insensibility to motives, we see, grows rapidly upon men. We see men, after leaving pious parents and homes, get further and further off from the best influence of their lives, until finally they laugh at all sacred things. I do not see fallen men restore themselves here, where everything helps restoration, and I cannot see how it can be there, where everything seems to hinder and forbid it. There is one unanswerable proposition to this whole idea of universal salvation. It is this : To save all is to save none."

"Well," said the skeptic, "(excuse me for saying it) you do have some very queer if not absurd ways of putting things."

"That may be," replied the preacher, "but a congeries of all sorts of animals in one cage do not seem to form a very happy community. The birds are not happy while the snake writhes around on the floor and fixes upon them its small, hungry, dreadful eyes; the monkeys are not happy when the porcupine moves. Every one is in each other's way ; all are unnatural, gloomy, without congeniality or possible companionship. Nobody is happy. A universal heaven is a universal hell, or, in other words, 'No hell, no heaven.' Salvation as a destiny is a necessity—a compulsion—something from which man cannot escape : in other words, a man is most unhappy when compelled to be happy."

"Well, then," was the reply,

2. "Let Man Achieve Salvation for Himself."

"That is impossible," replied the preacher, "for as long as God is God, he could not sell salvation, and as long as man is man, he could not buy it. God needs nothing that man has; besides, if it were not so, man has nothing that is not already God's. The gold and the silver, the cattle upon a thousand hills, the land, and all that we have and are already belong to God. If we cannot buy salvation with wealth, can we any more certainly achieve it by deeds? If so, whose deeds? There is none that doeth good; no, not one. No man was ever universally approved, or, other men being the judge, ever deserved salvation. 'The trail of the serpent is over all' we do. Out of the kind side of the heart may come a number of kindly acts, but out of the larger, weak, ignorant, vicious side will come many more wicked acts. A moral balance sheet of the life of humanity will show a hideous moral deficiency. A true human history would be nothing more or less than a police gazette of the race."

"You seem to be hard to please," said the skeptic. "You think it impracticable to save man by compulsion or destiny, or by arranging it so that he could not be lost if he would; and you put man down among the pauper class, as to the means of purchasing his safety, or you make the achievement of his salvation a moral failure, and I suppose you would equally object to his

3. "Salvation as a Gift."

"Not in the least," replied the preacher. "That is the only way, in my judgment, he can be saved. Salvation must be either a destiny, a human achievement either by purchase or deeds, or a gift. The constitution of the human mind requires it to be the last. To have heaven or salvation thrust on man by the compulsion of destiny, would seem to imply that he would not take it without such compulsion, either because he did not suit the place or because the place did not suit him. Heaven is no prison, nor are its inhabitants victims. And yet man would not buy a cheap heaven, nor thank God for one he himself had merited. Man cannot deserve the heaven that he desires, nor does he desire the heaven that he can deserve."

> 'T is clear, salvation's either thrust *on* man,
> Deserved *by* man, or won *for* man. How else?
> If thrust on man 't is thrust on some or all.
> If thrust on some 't is hard not thrust on all ;
> If thrust on all 't is thrust on none. 'T is plain,
> One place is not for all—no Hell, no Heaven.
> Deserved by man, salvation is a right,
> And as a right is not. We take, not earn.
> 'Gainst God, no rights, in guilt or innocence.
> 'T is won for man by Christ. He gives to men
> What neither men could buy nor God could sell,
> Or force upon acceptance. Other hope
> Is not, nor need for more in life or death.
> We choose the end, but God the means we use.
> If saved by Christ, then saved by Christ alone.
> By grace He saves through faith His offered gift.
> All deathless hopes hang on a deathless God.

> >   Both tares and wheat alike
> >   Drink in the sun ;
> >   The growth is base and good—
> >   The life is one.
> >   But when the Reapers come,
> >   They both shall fall ;
> >   And each its place shall take,
> >   Then endless all.

V.

The Skeptic as a Mourner.

"Good evening," said the preacher, as one day on his way home he met his friend, the skeptic. "I sympathize with you most sincerely, in your recent great affliction."

"Thank you, most kindly," returned the skeptic, offering his hand; "and I with you, sir."

"The sentiment of sympathy is itself a sorrow," said the preacher. "From the depths of my own affliction, I have thought of you often, and prayed to God that as your day so might be your strength."

"And is it so with you?" asked the skeptic. "Does all your faith compensate you for the loss of your child?"

"I should rejoice to know that you had as

much, in the loss of yours," replied the preacher. "To die is gain."

"Can you," asked the skeptic, with tearful eyes telling of the agony he would stoically conceal; "Can you, holding the dead form of your child in your arms, tell me that 'To die is gain'? Why do you attempt to comfort yourself with such thoughts? Death is inevitable, and men must bear what they cannot avert. How is death a gain? I ask from a grief I can neither express nor conceal."

By this time they had reached the home of the preacher. As it was a little on in the evening, his skeptical friend declined to go in, but accepted a chair, for a moment, on the open porch. The night was balmy and still. For a moment neither spoke, as they turned their eyes up to the jeweled dome above them. As our hearts are with our treasures, the thoughts of each were with the Silent Ones far away in the Invisible. There was no moon, but the stars were out in splendid dominion; and if Nature were God, both of these smitten men might have knelt in this Temple, built without hands, and have worshipped the Supreme Glory. The preacher first broke silence: pointing to the stars, he said :

"How came all these worlds here ?"

"You would not accept my theory," replied the skeptic.

"That theory," replied the preacher, "is from your head. This is the hour of your heart. What we wish to find in this world, around us, is not a constructive Principle, but a sympathizing Presence. The worlds have come, and we are to go."

"But where!" ejaculated the skeptic. "I have asked these stars, that look eternal; but they shine aloft in silence, unheeding of human agony."

"The Maker of the stars," said the preacher, "knows that our light afflictions, which are but for a moment, work out for us a far more exceeding and eternal weight of glory."

"And yet the stars, as heavenly lights in heavenly darkness, do answer you; teaching you love and reverence from afar."

"I have asked the winds to solve the mystery of life and death, but they hasten on their viewless paths, with a meaningless sigh from the great heart of nature."

"Is it meaningless? Do the winds in their circuits carry no message from zone to zone of the power and goodness of the mighty Superintendent?"

"Alas! when I look into the science of things, and remember that wind, which howls like an infinite fiend or sighs like a saint, is only fluent air sliding into a vacuum, my soul loses the thought of the beautiful, and nature becomes again a soulless fact."

"But is it soulless? If before the wind there is a vacuum to be filled, what is before the vacuum? Do you not believe in a Providence?"

"I have tried to believe, but cannot. I cannot suppose that God, if there be a God, would change his general laws, which are presumed to be of such perfect wisdom as neither to need nor to admit of change, because I requested him to do so to suit my wishes. What motive could I urge before him which was not before him at the first, to modify, in my behalf, his will as to all?"

"The motive is in himself, not in you."

"What is that?"

"His love."

"Did he not love me from the first?"

"You did not exist from the first."

"Did he not begin to love me, then, when I began to exist?"

"Certainly."

"Then why should he love me more when I pray to him, than at any other time?"

"Because you are more lovable."

"When I ask him to keep a ship, carrying my child, from foundering in a storm, I cannot suppose that he will interrupt the operation of a general law to grant my prayer."

"Let me ask you," said the preacher, "what is law?"

"I should like to hear *you* answer that."

"Then *law is will*. Will is one, as the sun;

law many, as the rays. As every ray is all sun, so is every law all will. The ship at sea in a storm is—"

"Under the operation of a general law, is it not?"

"Why is the wind blowing so fiercely?" asked the preacher.

"Because there is a vacuum to be filled."

"What makes the vacuum?"

"Heat."

"Why should heat make a vacuum?"

"Because it rarifies the air, and it rises."

"Why should rarified air rise?"

"Because it is lighter than unrarified air around it."

"Why should there be this difference in the gravity of air?"

"I do not know. Do you?"

"I believe," said the preacher, "that the general laws of the universe are only the general will of some Absolute Being. And law may change with the change of the will of the lawmaker. It is his will that heat should expand

and rarify the air—that rarified air shall rise above the colder and denser air—that colder air shall gravitate into the vacuum to fill it—that that movement of the air creates a current of wind—and that current may be rapid enough to rise from a wind to a whirlwind. All the way along, what you call law is only *will* at work. No one can say upon what motives He may vary the decisions of that will. We see a variation in the action of our own wills, and can understand how he could vary his. He may will that at the spot where the ship is there shall be a wall or mountain of cold air below, and a region of hot air above, and so curve the wind upward and over the ship, to fill the vacuum, toward which the wind moves."

"When," said the skeptic, "I have been alone with the thoughts of my precious dead, I have asked space in all of its illimitable fields to give me back my child. But there was no ear to hear, and no tongue to answer. On the surf-washed shore I have called her name, and been answered by the eternal requiem of the sea. I have challenged the darkness and invoked the light; 1 have climbed the solitary mountain and wandered in the sequestered vallies, but nature brings me no message from the dead. There is no God and no future. My child was, but is not. We are without power and without hope. We are nothing." The skeptic arose, and walked up and down, moved by his deep, intense agony. With his hands convulsively clenched, and heaving breast, he said: "I would, but cannot, strike this Nature that creates but to crush. I would tear her from her heartless throne, and stamp out her soul as she stamps out mine. Terrible, pitiless, remorseless power! In vain all fears have implored her to spare; in vain all loves have been sacrificed at her altar; in vain all hearts have broken at her feet. Nature is omnipresent, omnipotent, eternal Hatred. She loves and spares nothing. She never pauses, but on and on, the great Tomb-builder moves, without pity or remorse. Life is a doom. *Of all the past, nothing lives.* Nor shall anything live that is yet to come. The first breath presages the last. The bloom on the cheek invites the worm to its feast." He stopped, and though the stars still shone aloft, telling glorious things to all the world who could receive them, he looked hopelessly out into the dark; for Nature has no darkness like a darkened soul. Nature gave and Nature took away his child, annihilating its own gift. To him who had worshiped knowledge and sneered at faith, his child had ceased to be; and, even if immortal, dreadful death stood between them and before him. To curse was not to conquer his master. He stood despairing on the shore of an unlighted and unexplored ocean, awaiting the inky wave commissioned to sweep him into its unfathomable caverns of nothingness. Silently he offered his hand to the preacher, and walked away, without hope and without God in the world. The preacher entered the house and sought his closet, and, kneeling before the God of all comfort, prayed for light to the prayerless, and for strength to the weak.

In his own affliction, he himself reached on from the past to the future, from mortality to immortality, and all was peace.

When they next met, the skeptic was more composed, but not more resigned. He said to the preacher: "I have tried to believe as you do, but cannot. You trust in a Supreme Person, I see nothing but Supreme Power."

"With either at the head of the universe," was the reply, "you may have the comfort of future reunions with your dead. In all our conversations I have discussed with you upon the subject of

"Hell as a Certainty of Evolution.

"I now ask you to consider

"Heaven as a Certainty of Involution.

"Herbert Spencer defines evolution to be 'the integration of matter and the dissipation of motion.' But involution is before evolution, as matter must first involve integrating force before it can integrate, and motion dissipating force before it can dissipate. The thing environed precedes the environment. The soil was before the seed. Seeds are adapted to environment, and environment to the seed. We evolve hell from our own natures, and we involve heaven from the nature of another. The Nazarene said: 'No man can come to me except the Father, which sent me, draw him.' Evolution, primarily, is a process of development; involution, primarily, is a law of help. Evolution is what we let out; involution is what we take in. We go down of ourselves; we go up by help of another. Evil we inherit; good we acquire. In ourselves, which we evolve, we are weak. We are strongest who appropriate or absorb the strength of others. Every individuality of men and things is a sort of corporation sole, that aggregates the unity into itself as a group. Evolution is the least, as it unrolls only ourselves; involution is the greatest, as it appropriates the strength of others. Evolution and involution, in one sense, are the same, and one is as certain as the other. This is the only difference, if any: Evolution of evil goes on with the nature it has, under the help of evil environment. Involution of good implies, first, a taking in of something we did not have, as, for instance, a regenerating grace into our evil hearts, and then a going on with our new nature under the help of good environment. In other words, in evolution environment helps on the old; in involution, environment first renews and then helps on the new. Excuse me if I repeat my ideas in the effort to be understood. I have not asked you to trust and adore my God, but to look into the future by the light, however feeble, of your own science. Both evolution and involution open to us the gates of eternal life. Indeed, evolution is but one of God's ways of working in matter from within. Involution is God's way in matter from without. So involution is God's way of operating upon the spirit of man from above man. Man involves the spirit of God, and becomes a new creature. He continues to involve that spirit,

and continues to grow in his new character.
Evolving his own nature, he goes down. Involving more and more of his new nature, he
goes up. Still, as you do not yet accept the
conception of a Divine Person, let us take all
possible hope from the progressive energies of
a universal Power.

"We inherit evil; we acquire good. As
what we are not, is so infinitely more than what
we are, we grow by appropriating or by absorbing from our environment; and he grows the
most that appropriates or absorbs the most.
Eternal wretchedness is evolved from an evil
nature, by involving much evil and little good.
Eternal happiness is evolved from a renewed
nature, by involving little evil and much good.
Unconscious absorption of evil or conscious appropriation of good is the secret of soul-growth
in either direction. We become giants, if we
can add a giant's strength to our own. As
trees are tall by growing towards the sun that
warms them, so we grow Godward, just as we
take in, from our environment, God's life. We

are made up of everything around us, and we are that of which we have the most. Do not circumstances enter so largely into our characters, that we may say that character is the psychology of circumstance? Our responsibility coincides with the freedom and activity of will-power. How far circumstance coerces us, and how far we refuse to be coerced, is not always evident. All the links of the chain of remote and immediate cause are not in sight. We see not the attachment of their ends."

Both are illustrated in the parable of the field of the tares and the wheat. The tare had one nature, and the wheat another. Both grew side by side in the same soil, warmed by the same sun, and softened by the same rain. In every respect the environment was the same; but each absorbed according to its nature. The growth of one was good, the other evil. Therefore the first thing to be ascertained is, what is the nature of the object to be developed. The wheat will at once absorb or involve all its surroundings from above and below, and quicken into marvellously abundant and valuable life.

Wheat progresses as wheat, and tares progress as tares. Each nature assimilates the food according to its own laws, and suitable to itself.

Where we go depends upon what we are and what we take into ourselves. We are innately inclined to evil. If we take into our evil natures more evil than good, we make and go to hell, the finality of evil. If we take in more good than evil, and enough to eradicate that evil, we go to heaven, the finality of good. Some think that nature and environment are not distinct, as parallels, or associated as substance and shadow, but that they interact by inscrutable conditions of cause and effect, and effect and cause. Does the good soil *permit* or *cause* the seed to spring up? But if you cannot yet reach the conception of a Divine person, let us take all possible hope from the progressive energies of an universal power. All things tell me that to die is gain."

"Convince me of that," said the skeptic,

with the earnestness of a soul seeking the comfort of light, "and you will save me from madness. I would give the world, if it were mine, to believe that I can ever see my child again."

"Let us then become calm, and seek the truth for the sake of truth, as a sure anchorage for our sorely afflicted hearts."

"Most willingly," remarked the skeptic; "but do not take advantage of my weakness under bereavement, to commit me to the sway of feelings rather than principle. I would believe as you do, but cannot. My comfort, if any, must come from proofs, not feelings."

"Or rather from both," remarked the preacher. "You do not believe what you yourself prove. I do not propose to give any new principle, but only ask you to see the force of the many-sided principles you have already uttered. I understand you to hold, as the doctrine of evolution, that everything progresses forever."

"Most certainly," said the skeptic.

The preacher continued: "It is well that we

have gone somewhat over this ground already. *The law of progress* coming on from the unknown past, abiding in the present, and enacted for the future, is so complete, that no one presentation of it can exhaust its consideration. That which has been said will enable us the better to comprehend that which we are now to say.

"As a mourner, you have ceased to be the philosopher. Shakspeare says 'that one fire ceases with another's burning'; and while your heart has gone on, your head has stopped. You have already announced every principle I should use to lead you through science to the comfort I have through revelation, as well as science. You hold to a law of progress."

"Yes," replied the skeptic; "but do we understand this law alike? You state your views of this law, and I will say how far we agree or disagree."

"Then," said the preacher, "the universe is not a suicide. It tends to continue, not destroy itself. Matter persists, force persists, consciousness persists."

"Right here is the difficulty," replied the skeptic. "I believe in a law of progress. I believe in the persistence of matter, and in the persistence of force; but when I see consciousness leave the eyes of my child, and see a change so painful pass over the features and form of her body, I must admit its elements to persist, but I am compelled to see that her form is dissolved forever. It is this fact of my observation in which the unchangeable laws of science give me no hope."

"In other words," said the preacher, "dissolution of the body seems to destroy the individual."

"Yes."

"But remember that the individual body is not the personal soul. We see large minds and noble characters in small and most unattractive bodies, as if the soul had gotten into the wrong form."

"But when I see my child die, I see no soul depart, and have not the slightest evidence that anything more is to be expected. No soul is seen, none speaks. But, as I held the weak, suffering form of my dying child, I saw that when she ceased to breathe she ceased to know me. I saw no soul depart; none out of the body spoke to me then, none speaks to me now. If this is not annihilation, what is? I must understand in order to believe."

"I could satisfy you at once," answered the preacher, "if you believed in revelation; but as you do not yet, I must meet you on your grounds of material science and speculative philosophy, and answer you out of your own ideas. All experience, embodied or disembodied, is individual. The change at death is, as before said, a secret for each. You never saw the soul of your child in the body, and is it surprising that you have not seen it out of the body? She had several bodies during her life time, and she seemed to need one no more than another."

"But she always had a body of some kind."

"And has now. There is a natural body and there is a spiritual body. The natural body constantly changes; the spiritual body continues its identity."

"But what becomes," inquired the skeptic, "of the body that is buried? Prove to me that I shall again see the body of my child."

"You will see your child again, and no more doubt her real existence than you did under all the changes of this world. To see her in the spiritual body she took with her at death, will be satisfactory; and to see her in the natural body she left for burial, to be spiritualized at the resurrection, is a future event alone with God."

"But, it was a pale, emaciated, diseased, and exhausted body. Is it your faith that the same body, in the same wasted condition, is to be restored? If the identical body is to come out of the grave that went in, is the body of the blind to come out blind, the headless to come out headless? How about the bodies of infants and the misshapen? I would like to get your ideas on these points."

"You only ask the old questions: 'How are

the dead raised up?' and, 'With what bodies do they come?' Do you wish me to refer to revelation, or to confine myself to reasons from science?" asked the preacher.

"I care not, so long as you give me reasons, and not dogmas," answered the skeptic.

"Well, then," replied the preacher, "I will quote you what St. Paul says, and if it be contrary to reason, you can reject it : 'That which thou sowest is not quickened except it die. And that which thou sowest, thou sowest not that body that shall be, but bare grain, it may chance of wheat, or some other grain. But God giveth it a body as it hath pleased him, and to every seed his own body. All flesh is not the same flesh ; but there is one kind of flesh of man, another flesh of beasts, another of fishes, and another of birds. There are also celestial bodies, and bodies terrestrial ; but the glory of the celestial is one, and the glory of the terrestrial is another. There is one glory of the sun, and another glory of the moon, and another glory of the stars ; for one star differeth from another star in glory. So, also, is the resurrection of the dead. It is sown in corruption; it is raised in incorruption. It is sown in dishonor, it is raised in glory. It is sown in weakness, it is raised in power. It is sown a natural body, it is raised a spiritual body. There is a natural body, and there is a spiritual body.' "

"That you may have my difficulties fully before you," interrupted the skeptic, "let me say, that I can conceive of no relation between the body that dies and the one that is raised. There is no resurrection of the old body, if a new one is to come. If I understand you, you believe that at the resurrection a new body, in some way, is to come out of the old one. But I cannot see the relation between a body absolutely dead and a new one. The new must be a creation. If you put a grain of wheat in the ground, it carries life down into the ground with it, and the new wheat comes out of a living seed, not a dead one. But, in all this process there is uninterrupted continuance of life. There is no break in the chain of vital operations, and consequently we are not embarrassed at all on the score of the *relation* which the new plant bears to the old one. Although it undergoes a great change of form, and the numerical particles are in a state of constant transition, yet, so long as we keep our eye on the unbroken thread of life, as from the old living grain of wheat to the new, we have no hesitation in saying that there is a consistent sense in which it is the same plant." [1]

"It is impossible," replied the preacher, "to keep an eye on the thread of life at all. The transmission of life from one grain of wheat to another is as incomprehensible as the product of a new, powerful, glorious, and incorruptible body from the old, dead one, buried in weakness, dishonor, and corruption. The living grain of wheat has, in itself, no more self-raising power than the dead body of man. *Power comes to it in the ground.*"

"The power that comes," remarked the

[1] Bush on the Resurrection of the Body, p. 51.

skeptic, "may quicken into life a seed retaining the living principle within it, but not raise to life the dead body from which the living principle has departed."

"The seed," replied the preacher, "is not quickened except it die. '*In all cases,*' says Prof. Le Conte, '*vital force is produced by decomposition.*' The whole process of sprouting is a process of dying. Life continues itself, but changes and renovates the matter which it uses. Life seeks the dead, not the living. The minerals over which arose vegetable life, had no life in themselves."

"But the abstract principle I wish to establish is this: That power not inherent in matter can come to matter; and if one power can come, why not another? That power comes to matter *ab extra*, is one of the most universal certainties in existence; and the nearer the earth the more power comes. You know the law of matter to be, that the power of gravitation varies inversely as the square of the distance. That which may be light as a feather at

THE DEAD RAISED UP. 197

a given distance above the earth, may be heavy as a ton at its surface. As a body falls, rapidly increasing power meets it from the earth, and hastens its descent. Again, I ask, if matter can take one force, then why not another?"

"But," interrupted the skeptic, "the seed takes the power that helps the living principle within, but the dead human body has no living principle within to be helped by any power that can come to it."

"But," continued the preacher, "admit that when the grain of wheat is buried, it carries life down with it into the ground; remember that the life thus carried into the ground must die in the ground, before a new life can come out of the ground. Decomposition precedes the new life in the grain of wheat, as much as that of the human body. Will science reject, as incomprehensible, the raising up of a dead body to life, to be reunited to a soul with which it once had a history, and accept, as it must, the raising up of a living vegetable from a dead mineral with which it never had a previous connection or relation of any kind? Why should it be thought a thing incredible, with you, that life should rejoin the body? The incredible part is, that life ever took hold of dead matter at all, not that it should retake the hold after once having had it. If you reject one incomprehensibility, why not the other?"

"Because," replied the skeptic, "I see one to be a fact, but not the other."

"You see life, for the purpose of nutrition, relaxing its hold on matter, and retaking it every instant," replied the preacher. "You admit the incessant renewal of our bodies, matter and mind incessantly separating and uniting, some particles going and others coming; and yet the body remains ever identical."

"True, true," ejaculated the skeptic, "I must admit that there is nothing in the nature of things forbidding the living soul to disconnect itself from the matter of the dead body, and again to connect itself. But as to the body, what end is served thereby?"

"The perfectability of the body," answered the preacher. "For causes we need not pause to consider now, the body is weak, and therefore sickly and decaying. We say that sin did this—but to go on. Life seems, in the progress of what you call Nature, to break its hold to get a better one. Life is ever exalting itself, and holding its ascensions. We are to go on to perfection, from glory to glory. If this living soul drops the dead matter of the body, in corruption, it raises it up in incorruption. If it separates from it for a while in dishonor, it, as it were, compensates matter, by raising it in glory. If it lets the body fall in weakness, it will raise it in invincible power. If it parts from the body as a natural one, a thing of matter, it will take matter up finally and assimilate it with spirit. This is your way of evolution—*the law of progress.* The *relation* of living bodies as effects or products, from dead bodies or matter as cause, is an omnipotent fact, whether we comprehend it or not. It is a law that a living thing must die in one plane or sphere of existence in order to live in another. The body must be absolutely dead in order to live finally. Life drops a wretched body in order to pick it up again glorified. Nature goes back a little way to acquire momentum to go on for ever. Ever and ever, she breaks down in order to build up. As you value immortality, you must see your privilege in dying utterly, in no qualified but an absolute sense, that you may live the second life forever. There is no reversal of the law, all through the universe, there is nothing *quickened except it die.* The renewed connection between life and matter in the resurrected body is no greater mystery than the original connection between life and matter. Unless the material body die, there can no more be a new spiritual body than there can be new wheat without the death of the old."

But this doctrine teaches that death was a course or law of life in nature, sin or no sin," said the skeptic.

"What is death[1]?" asked the preacher.

[1] "There is no death: what seems so is transition."—*Longfellow.*

"In sin or holiness this world was not man's home. Here we have no continuing city, says one. Sin has brought death as a penalty, as it is now here, into our world. But in perfect holiness, man without death as we now understand it, must have gone on to a more spiritual nature and home, for flesh and blood cannot inherit the Kingdom of God. We have so far come on through a series of material spheres of mineral, vegetal, and animal, and the next ascension is into a purer and less gross condition of existence. Without sin man would have been changed to suit his new sphere ; but the change would have been not as a purification, but as natural and welcome. On account of sin, we seem to throw off our material nature differently from what would have been necessary in a state of holiness. Our understandings are darkened. Besides, purification is needed. Life drops our material bodies, stained with sin, and takes them up at last with new power, superior to sin.

" If," said the skeptic, " death quickens the

grain of wheat and man's resurrection-body into life, why does it not quicken the body of the dead brute into a new life and body? If death gives life in one case, why not in all?"

"Death," replied the preacher, "quickens nothing. It is in the appointment of your evolutionary power, that nothing is quickened *except* it die, but not because it dies. By this power, all quickening from death to life is obedience not to death, but to the law of progress. This Power, or Nature, if you prefer so to call it, works upwards in terraces, not on levels. Life from death in the grain of wheat is an expansive movement from one to many. The life of the resurrection-body of conscious man is a progressive movement from corruption to incorruption, from dishonor to glory, from weakness to power, from a natural body to a spiritual body."

"Why should the body of the brute be excepted from the benefit of that law of progress?"

"Because nature does not care for all things

alike. She cares more for the strong than for the weak; she cares more for the fruitful than for the barren; she cares more for the conscious than the unconscious."

"But, you say she cares for the unconscious grain of wheat?"

"Yes; for, in caring for the unconscious wheat, she cares for the conscious man. Nature ever keeps the best in view. Conscious man is at the top of things, and all below are his supporters. Everything, directly or indirectly, is to help him. Ceasing to help, they cease to be. Man continues because, as we have said, consciousness, like force and matter, is an independent and imperishable substance. But the brute belongs not to the order of conscious beings. Man drops his body at death, in order, according to the law of progress, to take up a better one at the resurrection."

"When is that?"

"It matters not, so that there be a resurrection. Any time should satisfy us."

"Where is the body until the resurrection?"

"Wherever nature can best keep it."

"Where is that?"

"The Great Power answers: 'What I do thou knowest not now, but thou shalt know hereafter.' You may be answered to-morrow, to-day, this hour. An answer you will be sure to get, and in an hour ye think not. That we are to exist personally is a certainty, either in bodies now unknown to us, or in our old ones, renovated and restored to us. If we do not get back these old bodies, we shall not need or miss them; and if we do, we shall be satisfied with them. Continued existence is all I ask, in the body or out of it. I could expound to you the doctrines of the Bible as to a spiritual body, the one that met Christ in Paradise, on the day of the Crucifixion, but—"

"At present," said the skeptic, "let us keep to the purely scientific or philosophical argument, as the one in which I am more at home. If you can show me that, in the nature of things, there is this future to the soul and this resurrection of the body, we may then consult what are claimed as authoritative and inspired revelations of its character. You have given me your argument from my ground of nature, as to the fact and character of a future hell; but I should be more gratified to find you make as good an argument in favor of a future heaven."

"The line of *a priori* argument, or from cause to effect, is the same. The law of progress necessitates a heaven as much as a hell. The only difference is this : we sink to hell by the gravitating evil inherent in ourselves. We are lifted into heaven by a grace imparted to us, or by environment, keeping to scientific terms.

I claimed before that human nature was a fallen thing, and needed not only to be helped up, but to be constantly held up. Of itself, it would gravitate lower and lower into evil. In religious teaching, we would call this help a divine grace. You would call it a law of progress. As the nature of man, affected, if not vitalized, by environment, makes a hell the necessity of law; so his nature, changed by environment into a new nature, but with unchanged personality, affected, if not continuously vitalized, by environment, makes a heaven by the necessity of law. Nature and circumstance are omnipotent in either direction."

"Of course," remarked the skeptic, "in this heaven of yours, you hold that we shall know each other, as we did here. You expect to meet there and to know your daughter again?"

"Yes, as you may yours," replied the preacher.

> 'Is *ignorance* found in the spirit's home?
>   Is *memory* left in the dust?
> Then shall we not feel that we stand alone,
>   As strangers among the just?
> And can it be so, in that city of light,
> Where love is unfailing and joy ever bright?"
> Is darkness found in that cloudless sky,
>   Veiling the life just past?
> Forgotten the friend who saw us die,
>   All faithful and true to the last?
> And can it be so? Shall we meet no more
> When this feverish dream of life is o'er?'

"No, no, my friend, this world is not all. One world no more excludes another than one moment excludes another, or a cause excludes an effect. I expect another world hereafter, because I have already had one here. And that world will supplement this.

> 'Go, wing thy flight from star to star,
> From world to luminous world, as far
> As the universe spreads its flaming walls;
> Take all the pleasures of all the spheres,
> And multiply each through endless years—
> One minute of heaven is worth them all.'

"The Peri caught only a glimpse of the glorious reality. The eye hath not seen, nor the ear heard, nor hath it entered the heart to conceive the good things that God hath reserved for those who love Him. And all this is to be under the law of progress. If you live, and move, and have your being under law, you must ever continue under law; and that law is one of progress in good or evil, forever and ever. I know no reason why existence should cease. This law of progress necessitates a heaven. And that same law necessitates that heaven shall eternally become more heaven, as hell must eternally become more hell. 'The mechanical axiom,' says Spencer, 'that, if left to itself, matter moving in any direction will continue in that direction with undiminished velocity,' is a law for mind as well as matter, for the future as well as the present, for heaven as well as for hell, for good as well as for evil."

"These," said the skeptic, "are truths that convince my head, but how can I make them interest my heart?"

."By forming new mental habits," replied the preacher. "Pray to the Great Being behind all nature. Instead of educating yourself to doubt, seek for thoughts that honor Him. When you grasp a law of the universe, forget not the Lawgiver."

Days, weeks, months passed—sorrow keeps no record of time—and when they next met, the mourning skeptic greeted the preacher warmly, and said: "When I reached my home, after our last conversation, I opened a Bible that had been closed for years, and by a singular coincidence, I opened at this sentence: 'Lord I believe; help Thou mine unbelief.' Somehow, that prayer lingers in my mind wherever I may be. It seems philosophical, that increasing knowledge should enlighten and deepen belief. Everywhere is the law of repair—call it mercy, if you choose. But mercy requires One Merciful. I confess, that to conceive this universe to be directed and managed by an Infinite Person is no less logical, and immeasurably more comforting, than to believe it to be only the evolutionary work of an Impersonal Power. If there can be a Power, there can be a Person, a Governor, a Judge, a Friend, a Redeemer, A CHRIST."

The two clasped each other's hands, as the one holy light of knowledge and faith rested in their hearts, and illuminated, for both, the same deathless future. By that light, each heart bent a longing gaze across the Dark River, and tears of joy moistened their eyes, as they saw their children standing in joy on the other side, with their beautiful hands outstretched to the loved ones on this, beckoning them on to

THE ETERNAL SHORE.

www.ingramcontent.com/pod-product-compliance
Lightning Source LLC
Chambersburg PA
CBHW031814220426
43662CB00007B/644